The Baseball Whisperer

THE
Baseball
WHISPERER

A Small-Town Coach Who Shaped
Big League Dreams

MICHAEL TACKETT

Houghton Mifflin Harcourt
BOSTON   NEW YORK
2016

For information about permission to reproduce selections from this book, write
to trade.permissions@hmhco.com or to Permissions, Houghton Mifflin Harcourt
Publishing Company, 3 Park Avenue, 19th Floor, New York, New York 10016.

www.hmhco.com

Library of Congress Cataloging-in-Publication Data

Names: Tackett, Michael.
Title: The Baseball Whisperer: a small-town coach who shaped
Big League dreams / Michael Tackett.
Description: Boston : Houghton Mifflin Harcourt, 2016.
Identifiers: LCCN 2015037778 | ISBN 9780544387645 (hardcover) |
ISBN 9780544386396 (ebook)
Subjects: LCSH: Eberly, Merl. | Baseball coaches — United States — Biography. |
Baseball — Iowa — Clarinda.
Classification: LCC GV865.E3 T33 2016 | DDC 796.357092 – dc23
LC record available at http://lccn.loc.gov/2015037778

Printed in the United States of America
DOC 10 9 8 7 6 5 4 3 2 1

Frontispiece photograph courtesy of
Nodaway Valley Historical Museum Archives, Clarinda, Iowa

For Julie, Kate, and especially Lee,
the player who refused to give up

Contents

The Baseball Whisperer

Foreword

MERL EBERLY CREATED a real-life *Field of Dreams*. From his small town of Clarinda, Iowa, he built a national baseball powerhouse that produced three dozen major leaguers, including a Hall of Famer, and more than three hundred players who signed professional contracts. He helped to develop thousands of others, not just to become better players but also better people. He did it with the help of the people of his hometown, his tireless and relentlessly optimistic wife and partner, Pat, and the family-like community that baseball can be. He worked on his dream for more than fifty years, never asking anything in return and never receiving a dime for his labors. He did it to provide opportunity, to teach life lessons, and to stay connected to the game he loved. A coach had rescued him, and Merl spent his adulthood doing the same for others.

For many players, college summer ball represents the final chance to get a shot at playing professionally. They play with wooden bats to replicate the experience of pro ball and hope a scout will be sitting in the stands on the night they are at their best. The schedules are intense, sixty games over two months, and the bus rides between towns can be five or six hours long. Teams are located in hamlets such as Butler, Pennsylvania; New Market, Virginia; St. Joseph, Missouri; and Liberal, Kansas. They provide the towns with a sense of purpose and belonging, and they also deliver a low-cost source of entertainment. Host families open their homes to players, providing surrogate parenting, transportation, and cheerleading along with free room and board. In Clarinda, Merl Eberly also tried to find summer jobs for the players, whether it was running a jackhammer, sweeping factory floors, or painting the outfield fence.

Clarinda, a town of five thousand people located in the southwestern corner of the state, two hours from anywhere, is one of the smallest of those small places with a major college summer team. I know because my family lived it.

Our son made it to the college ranks, only to be cut during his sophomore year. He was devastated, yet refused to give up, writing to one hundred summer teams to ask for a chance. Only one of them said yes: the Clarinda A's. It was during that summer that I learned a wonderful story about baseball and an even better one about life.

The Baseball Whisperer is the tale of a man, a town, and a team. It is the story of Merl Eberly, whose life was touched by a coach when he was a teenager headed for trouble. Instead, he became a standout athlete, playing four sports. His best was baseball, and he got his shot at the pros.

But this story is about much more than baseball. It is a narrative about a small-town America that people think lives only in myth. Players come to Clarinda from all over the country to find out how good they are on the field and what kind of men they will become. Eberly dedicated his life to providing opportunity for thousands of young men, all chasing the same dream he had harbored. He and the people of Clarinda changed lives. They did it without a glamorous setting or a lavishly funded program. They did it with their sweat and their hearts.

Merl Eberly, the quiet hero next door, was able to build a network of college coaches and pro scouts and then attract players from some of the highest-caliber collegiate baseball programs. These players come from manicured fields and fancy clubhouses to Municipal Stadium, where cornfields line the right-field fence, local businesses buy billboard ads in the outfield, and the county fair livestock pens sit across the street.

The players who make the trip learn about more than baseball, and that too was part of Eberly's plan. He wanted to help young players become better men, learn the value of discipline and the selflessness of team play. He was stern. He demanded 100 percent effort, and when he didn't get it, he would require punishing runs along the town's bypass or endless loops in the outfield. Eberly admired George Patton and John Wayne and shared some traits with both men. He had standards and did not make exceptions for players who considered themselves above the team. While he was tough, he was never physically abusive and didn't resort to profanity to make his point. Players also came to learn that he was demanding for their sake, not to feed his own ego. They discovered a softness and kindness beneath the tough façade. He found a way to tell players to trust their skills as he built their confidence, along with a lifelong kinship. "It's not about can we make them a better baseball player," Merl said. "It's about can we make them a better person." Some of the most famous coaches in college baseball became his disciples.

The town of Clarinda is a fitting place for an open embrace from people like Merl Eberly. Clarinda first opened its arms to slaves fleeing Missouri, and then to more than a dozen homeless children who were transported from Eastern cities to the Midwest in the Orphan Train Movement of the nineteenth and early twentieth centuries. Clarinda is a place where values and commitment matter: for instance, the city council rejected a Wal-Mart for fear that it would change the town's character by driving local merchants out of business.

The families and the players they host for the summers create enduring relationships. Some players have met their bride in Clarinda and also made their home there. Many write faithfully every year — even those who went on to the majors — sending holiday greetings and birthday cards to their "moms" and "dads."

Merl Eberly was the heartbeat of Clarinda and a baseball whisperer, little known outside his town except to a circle of coaches, scouts, and the players and families who spread his legend. Players coming to get their shot left with much more, schooled not only in the game by Eberly but also in decency by the town collectively. In a sport that is dominated by money and cynicism and often treats players as mere commodities, Merl Eberly stood in opposition, forming citizen-athletes who carried a moral compass that he had instilled in them. He could have done it to make money, like those running dozens of other teams around the country. Instead, he invoked one rule for Clarinda management and coaches: nobody got paid. All funds went toward the players and the program.

Merl Eberly coached for more than four decades and served as his team's general manager until his death in June 2011. The players who passed through Clarinda went on to become fixtures on *SportsCenter* and magazine covers, and they populate major league rosters and World Series play to this day.

I arrived in Clarinda, Iowa, like most people, driving along Glenn Miller Avenue, past the museum dedicated to the town's most famous son, the renowned bandleader. My destination, Municipal Stadium, was less than a mile away. I was going there to see Eberly. Our son, reeling from being released by his college team only a few weeks before, was in the middle of an athletic and personal trial and renewal. He had written Merl and Pat Eberly, laying out his desire and asking for a chance. Merl was skeptical of a player who had been released. But Pat reread the letter and asked, "Isn't this just the kind of player we want here?"

The experience was restorative, both on the field and off. Our son's host family, Jill and Mike Devoe, who lived ten miles outside of Clarinda in a town of five hundred people, opened their home and their hearts to him, a kid who had grown up in metropolitan Washington, DC. Clarinda showed him a part of the country and an aspect of humanity that he had never seen. On the field, he proved he could compete on an even higher level. Upon his return to school, he made the team and became one of its top pitchers. More important, his faith in people was renewed.

The Baseball Whisperer recounts part of a journey that some parents make with their children all over the United States. It starts with that first baseball glove before Little League and goes on through travel teams and high school teams, the pyramid narrowing with each step. Some players move to the college ranks, still hoping that their days on the field won't end yet. Playing in the summer, with wooden bats like the pros, they try to prove to scouts and coaches that they have what it takes.

Summer baseball programs offer an internship in life, one that pays in ways other than money. Clarinda is one of the smallest towns with such a successful program, and it works because the people of Clarinda represent a set of American values that we tend to think exist only in our nostalgia-driven imaginations.

In a time of increased specialization in sports, with travel leagues starting at ever-earlier ages, private coaches, and intense schedules, the program sustained for so many years by Merl and Pat Eberly still thrives because it honors the essence of the game and the best traits that players bring to a team.

When I met Merl and Pat Eberly and saw firsthand what they had built, when I watched a game at that stadium, with silos in the distance and corn as high as the right-field fence, I was convinced that they had created something that went well beyond baseball.

1

Changed Lives

WHEN PAT EBERLY woke up that morning and looked out at the gray skies and misty rain, she was alone for the first time in fifty-seven years. She had known this day was coming for at least a couple of years, though that didn't really make it any easier. Merl, whom she had known since elementary school, the father of their six children, had died in this room in their home at 225 East Lincoln Street, and the void brought a singular kind of pain. The cancer that had been diagnosed in 2007 had finally, four years later, sapped his strength and ability to fight it. Though Merl never liked losing, this battle had been unwinnable.

When Pat rose from the bed, each step around the room brought another memory. She had moved the bed she had shared with her husband to the north wall from the west, where it had been for half a century, just enough of a change to make it bearable to stay in the room. She looked at the miniature grandfather clock on the wall, the one that a former player, Mike Kurtz, had given them, made from a cherry tree cut down on

Kurtz's farm in Oregon, Missouri. The pendulum of the clock was still swinging, but the hands had stopped at the time Merl's body was taken from the house.

On the landing of the second floor outside the bedroom, Merl would do calisthenics first thing each morning, a series of jumping jacks, push-ups, and sit-ups. Heading down the steps, she could hear the groans of the old oak stairs, born of all those years of him running up and down for exercise or listening for one of the kids to come home at night. She would later decide to hang the large portrait of Merl at the bottom of the stairs. Her children questioned the decision, but came to agree that it was the best place for it because that was where Merl would stand to call up to them, mimicking "reveille" or shouting "Time to do chores" or "Quiet down up there."

When Pat turned into the dining room, it was like walking into a museum of their life together, a time dominated by their love of baseball and family. She stood there, looking at their life's work in the dozens of photos hanging on each wall. There were pictures of the men who had become major league baseball players, like Hall of Fame shortstop Ozzie Smith, Philadelphia Phillies star Von Hayes and Buddy Black, an All-Star left-handed pitcher who went on to be manager of the San Diego Padres. Smith's place on the wall was special, and one striking color photograph in particular underscored how deep their relationship was. It showed Smith midway through his signature backflip at the Baseball Hall of Fame in Cooperstown, New York, a display of athleticism that had endeared him to fans and his teammates. The lighting, the focus, and the contrast were all perfect, and it looked like a photo from a magazine. In fact, that is what it was. The photo was scheduled for the cover of *Sports Illustrated* to note Smith's entry into the Hall of Fame, but never appeared because Ted Williams had died that week. The editors chose to put Williams on the cover instead. The photo was signed by Smith, one of only two copies.

Most of the photographs were inscribed to "Merl and Mrs. E." The players had come during college summers from across the country to a place most had never heard of, Clarinda, Iowa, to play for a man whose reputation had been spread through word of mouth by players, coaches, and scouts, a whispered kind of fame.

Another wall was reserved for photos of the family, featuring the three sons wearing the uniforms of three different professional teams, posed as players do for baseball cards, and their three daughters, including an exhausted Jill breaking the tape after winning a race just as her father had taught her to finish — with no effort left to give.

Enough reflecting, Pat thought, and promptly got busy, the only way she knew how to be and the only way she was going to get through this day. She went through the checklist in her head. She had always been the detail person in her partnership with Merl. She wanted her husband's body dressed in his gray suit and his favorite baseball-dotted tie. For the floral arrangement for the casket, she chose roses. Merl had sent her roses each year for their anniversary, one for every year of their marriage. The previous October he had sent a total of fifty-six. For this day she wanted one red rose to represent her, six white ones for their children, eleven pink ones for the grandchildren, and five yellow baby roses for the great-grandchildren. She even made a seating chart for special guests at the funeral service, then laughed to herself about her obsessiveness.

Rick, their oldest son, had been up since 5:30 after a sleepless night. He drove in the dawn's light to the family timber hunting ground, about five miles from his boyhood home. The orange sunrise began to pour up from the broad horizon, the way it does in the middle of the country. He walked the fence line to gather himself, saw clouds forming, and hoped there would be no rain. The woods had been a special place for him and his father; for more than a half-century, they had bonded there while hunting pheasant or deer or fishing nearby. They could talk the whole time or not say a word, and the experience was almost the same. They were only twenty-two years apart, so their relationship was particularly close. A rooster pheasant crowed in the distance, announcing the morning and reminding Rick he had to head back.

The family had decided to hold a private burial before the funeral so that the service could be a celebration of Merl's life. A limousine was parked on the east side of the house to lead a procession of cars to the cemetery, behind a police escort. As the family gathered in the caravan, Joy, the fourth of the six children, still couldn't really take in the fact that she would never hear that voice again, the one saying, "There's my baby girl," or, "Hey, kiddo," whenever she saw him. Even worse, she would never feel the warmth and strength of the bear hugs Merl gave her, with those huge hands, hands that always made her feel safe. They were also the hands that administered punishment, but embraces far outweighed spankings. When she held them one last time, she didn't want to let go.

Joy's three brothers and Merl's six oldest grandsons raised the casket into the hearse, each wanting to make sure he had a hand in lifting Merl's body. When they arrived at the gravesite, rain started to fall more steadily. "Tears from heaven," Jill said. The minister read a passage from the Bible. Pat and her six children sat in chairs near other family members and a few close friends, including Smith, Hayes, and Jose Alvarez, another alumnus of the Clarinda A's who went on to star in the major leagues, stood under a tent. They touched the casket before it was lowered, then returned to the cars to drive to the church.

They entered the side door of St. John's Lutheran Church and headed to the basement to regroup. Pat had thought they would have the service in the family church, Westminster Presbyterian, which had a capacity of just over two hundred, but her children finally persuaded her that it would be much too small. Their baseball family was too large. It was good advice. The larger church was packed with mourners, who filled the sanctuary's choir loft, the adjoining chapel, and the balcony; in fact, a video hookup was needed in the basement to accommodate the overflow crowd.

As Pat scanned the pews each person triggered a separate memory. The central themes of the life she'd had with Merl were all there in one place — the man, the town, and the team that they built.

As they waited in the basement they were joined by three former professional players who credited their time in Clarinda with launching their careers. There was Smith, the former shortstop for the St. Louis Cardinals, who had come to Clarinda in the summer of 1975 as a player with promise, waiting for his opportunity to play for the team that Merl managed, the Clarinda A's. Smith arrived as a 140-pound, five-foot-nine-inch shortstop who had been ignored by Division 1 college teams and professional scouts. It took one session of hitting ground balls to Smith for Merl to see a talent that others did not.

Von Hayes was there too. He had played twelve years in the

major leagues and was once traded for five players. He came to Clarinda in 1978, only to be intimidated by the skill of the other players. He asked Merl to release him and to consider giving him a chance the following year. Merl agreed to let him come back — he always had a soft spot for kids with genuine desire. Hayes returned the following summer, and within two years he was playing in the big leagues.

Alvarez also stood among them. After playing for Eberly, Alvarez went on to pitch for the Atlanta Braves, and more than twenty years later he saw his son, Seve, play center field in Clarinda. For Alvarez, Eberly filled the hole left by an absent father who never came to see his son play in the big leagues. "Merl told me, 'One summer in Clarinda will change your life,'" Alvarez said in his eulogy. "And in so many ways, it really did — because of Merl."

Merl's impact on these professional players at a formative time in their lives stands in such contrast to the caricature of the entitled athlete. Their time with him engendered a sense of mutual friendship and obligation that would outlast playing careers, some marriages, and fame.

Other players, spanning six decades of baseball in Clarinda, were waiting to join the Eberly family in the church. Merl had been so proud of these men who came to Clarinda as boys, especially the ones who had come the furthest and made something of themselves, perhaps because they reminded him of himself, a man who a lot of people thought would never amount to anything.

Townspeople who had helped Merl sustain his team were there as well. Families who had opened their homes to players to live for the summer, to watch over them, feed them, and cheer them, people like Mike and Jill Devoe, were there. Jill's parents had hosted A's players when she was a child, giving her summer "big brothers," and she and Mike went on to do the same, giving their own children the experience of taking someone into their home, providing support and comfort, expecting nothing in return. Owners of many of the small businesses in town whose contributions over the years kept the program alive, like Larry and Shira Bridie, came as well. The Bridies ran Weil's, a clothing store on the town square that often provided the uniforms for Merl's Clarinda A's. They gave Merl money, they hosted players, they attended the games, and they wholeheartedly bought into Merl's dream of what the team could do for the town. Former classmates from Clarinda High School, including those who never thought Merl's marriage to Pat would last, sat among the crowd. Colleagues from the *Clarinda Herald-Journal* were there too, including the people who hired Merl back in the 1950s. Merl would spend thirty years writing and selling ads for the *Herald-Journal*.

Then there were the baseball people, the scouts, the coaches, along with the men affiliated with major league teams and executives from the National Baseball Congress (NBC). They couldn't miss this moment to honor a man who embodied for them baseball's most virtuous dimensions, like trust and honor and the spirit of what it means to be part of a team.

When the family walked up the stairs, they saw a crowd of six hundred people who had come to honor Merl. Ryan, the sensitive, broad-shouldered middle son who had taken over coaching the team a few years after Merl stepped down, looked around the church and took a measure of the lives his father had touched, the people who felt compelled to travel from across the country to pay their respects. He had been a part of his father's dream from his days as an A's batboy to his signing of a professional contract with the New York Yankees, to his return as the man who would replace his father on the field as the manager. When his other family members spoke and sang at the service, he thought about how strong his father had made all of them.

The two oldest great-grandsons wore their Cubs jerseys to honor Merl's favorite team — her dad had always loved an underdog, Joy remembered. He had listened to the Cubs on the radio as a child, then on the superstation WGN with Harry Caray delivering the play-by-play, the team's futility never quite pathetic enough to override Merl's loyalty.

The family lined up for seating in order of age, according to Pat's chart. The six children and their families sat with Pat in the front pews on both sides. A large photo of Merl was placed on an easel. The entire Clarinda A's team from 2011, each wearing the team jersey, stood along the south wall so others could sit. This was not a part of Pat's script. The players came up with the idea — and the emotional impact was powerful. Just the sight of them made Joy weep. Her husband, Dave Cox, would cry later, sitting in his truck, tears streaming down his face. "It makes you feel really selfish after hearing about all he did for others," he said of his father-in-law. "He really made a difference."

To Julie, the oldest child, the service took on a sense of the surreal, as though she were hearing the story of a man she did not know, someone whose quiet yet profound effect on others was in evidence all around her. Her mind returned to family times, Merl singing in the car on Sunday drives, playing ball with the kids in the yard, cranking ice cream by hand on the back porch, turning the handle until the sweat rolled off his nose. When there was a small glitch in the service music, she remembered him telling her before her first piano recital that if she made a mistake, just to keep on going. She did. She listened to her father. He gave her words she lived by.

Sitting nearby, Rod, Merl's youngest boy, and the one who most closely resembled him in strength and size, felt unable to release the overwhelming love and grief inside. He had the carefree manner of the "baby" in the family and was probably subject to the least discipline from Merl. Like his brothers, he too signed a professional baseball contract and probably had more potential than the others to make it to the majors. It didn't work out, though, and he found himself again using Clarinda as an anchor for his life. When he saw the players in their uniforms lining the wall of the sanctuary, he couldn't hold back. "I was ready for everything but that sight," he said. For the first time since his father's death, he cried.

Speaking for the family was grandson B. J. Windhorst, a handsome, six-foot-four man with a square jaw and a large chest, a gifted athlete who played college basketball at Drake University before a successful coaching career. He gathered himself. He had done plenty of public speaking, but nothing like this.

B.J. drew himself to full height, pulled back his shoulders, and took a deep breath. He said that whenever he was faced with a difficult decision, he would ask himself what Merl would think. Merl taught his players and his family a certain way of doing things that was not just about wins and losses, though Merl loved to win. B.J. counted ten things he thought Merl stood for. Among them: Love is not just a hug. Sometimes you have to tell people you love a hard truth. Sports provide a venue for learning. And "family always comes first, but a close second is the A's."

Cooper Eberly, Merl's five-year-old grandson, had inspired his mother, Rick's wife Angie, to write a poem, "Through My Eyes," which she read. Angie and Rick had waited seventeen years for a child, and Cooper held special status even in this large clan. The poem recounted Merl talking to Cooper about his illness and death. "That was the last time Grandpa talked to me, but I had more to say even though his eyes were closed. I'd give him play-by-plays."

Other former players who had become coaches, like Jeff Livin, had come this day as well. To honor the man who had shaped his life, Livin had driven 750 miles to Clarinda — twelve and a half hours — from Lufkin, Texas, where he was baseball coach at Angelina College. Livin had played for two seasons at Clarinda, starting out as a frightened kid with some talent, leaving as a player who would soon sign a professional contract. When his playing days ended, he became a coach. Livin counted Merl as one of the two most important men in his life, along with his father. He couldn't help regretting that Merl would no longer be there to pick up the phone as he had done so many times when Livin reached out to him when he was struggling. Livin thought he needed to be strong for others, but "then the finality of it hits you . . . and it's hard as hell."

It seemed like half the town was in the church too. Merl's boyhood friends were there, his teachers, his classmates, and the business owners he had persuaded so many times to write checks and keep the Clarinda A's alive. The troubled rural economy put strains on the team to the point where it almost folded many times. But through Pat's fastidious bookkeeping and Merl's relentless selling, they stayed afloat.

Dr. Bill Richardson, a family physician in Clarinda, rose to the lectern to speak about the impact of Merl's discipline and what a powerful motivator he could be. As a young track star, Richardson competed in the state finals and finished a disappointing fifth in the 440-yard dash, behind two runners he had defeated just the week before. Merl criticized Richardson's effort. "There was no question about the disdain he held for my performance," Richardson told the mourners. "I was crushed. How was it that this man I looked up to could be so harsh . . . I finally realized Merl couldn't stomach any athlete who didn't leave it all on the ball field or the track." Richardson said he made certain that would never happen again and often thought about Merl's criticism when he was studying late into the night, poring over chemistry and biology books, making sure that he did everything he could to be in a position to be accepted to medical school.

Richardson and his wife later served as house parents for the Clarinda A's for twenty years. In 1981 they hosted a pitcher from California named Cas Soma, one of the team's stars. Near the end of the season, Merl told Soma it was time to go home because he didn't think Soma was giving his full effort. Two weeks later, the A's won the national championship of the National Baseball Congress in Wichita, Kansas, while Soma was back in California, unable to listen to or watch the game. He learned the same lesson as Richardson. Soma continued his premed studies and went on to become a successful orthopedic surgeon in Hawaii. "Thanks to Merl and tough love," Richardson said.

Richardson also told the story of Jamey Carroll, an infielder who was told by Merl upon his arrival: "God didn't give you a lot of talent. If you are going to make it to the next level, you've got to hustle." Carroll would go on to do just that. "I was watching the Dodgers on television and said, 'Isn't it just amazing how Jamey can hit a routine grounder and run as if the devil is on his heels,'" Richardson said.

As a doctor, Richardson saw Merl in his office at least every three weeks near the end of his life, more as friend than physician. Richardson had a family practice, and Merl had an advanced form of cancer. "We'd sit and talk about former players, baseball and the A's, and his concerns about how you keep the program going with such budget problems. Merl didn't need to come and see me every two or three weeks. But I had to see Merl."

When news of Merl's decline and death became known, Pat was flooded with letters from former players, coaches, scouts, and even the umpires with whom Merl often feuded. Fifty once arrived on a single day. One letter written by a player from the East Coast was read at the funeral.

I wanted to write this letter to truly let you know how much last summer meant to me. When I arrived in Clarinda I was a broken person. Being cut from my college team left me searching for answers. It got me into bad habits ... You welcomed me with open arms and became one of the few people that showed faith and still believed in me. Your influence extended beyond the ball field as your familial and Christian values resonated with me. Slowly, I came to return to the person that I wanted to be. Without the opportunity that you presented me, I don't know where I would be. I am certain, without Clarinda, I wouldn't have made my college team, which would have left me stuck on the wrong path. Now I am securely on my college team with improved grades and a far more positive outlook on myself and my life. None of this would have been possible without you and your family. You are truly one of the more impressive men I have ever met because you have achieved genuine happiness not through exorbitant wealth but rather through a close-knit family, a steadfast belief in the Lord and by helping others achieve their goals. I will never forget or take for granted the opportunity you gave me.

Jose Alvarez spoke on behalf of former players. He had come to Clarinda for one reason in the summer of 1977: to pitch in front of professional scouts and get his shot after his college career at the University of Louisiana at Lafayette. "I run a tight ship here," Merl told him. "I can promise you will get better if you work hard. If you want to party and play around, this is not the place for you." Alvarez instantly took to the program, and Merl was right. After only a month in Clarinda, Alvarez was signed by the Atlanta Braves. "I was raised without a dad and quickly found out how Mr. E became a surrogate father to so many people . . . Mr. E taught me about values, such as cutting your hair, shining your shoes, showing up on time. He presented us with the challenges of living with those disciplines, things that many people deep down longed for . . . I remember him watching me pitch and wanting to impress him and make him proud . . . I remember walking out of a big league stadium and seeing Mr. E and Mrs. E there, something my dad never did. I remember how proud he was of guys whether they made it to the big leagues, medical school, or became umpires. He had an impact on our lives."

One of Merl's granddaughters, Jara Johnson, and his son-in-law John Brummett sang during the service. Jara later would finish writing a song honoring Merl entitled "Beyond the Field." She had played part of the song for him before his death, including the refrain, "Don't treat this life like a game you can make up someday. Don't play that way because beyond the field your riches lay."

There were equal parts tears and laughter during the service — probably about the right mix, as Merl wasn't one to cry. Pat, every bit as important to the A's program as her husband, wasn't either. She led the mourners out of the church, imperturbable as usual, showing little emotion. Then she saw the A's players and those from Clarinda High School, also in their uniforms, lining the front steps. Finally, she too broke down.

It hit Ozzie Smith the same way. It had been thirty-six years since he had first set foot in Clarinda and found out how far he could go in baseball, thanks to a man who believed in him. Merl had been passing on some form of that lesson ever since. Smith did not forget either Clarinda or the Eberlys over the years, and in many ways their relationship only grew deeper. In the young men lining the side of the church Smith could see himself more than three decades earlier. "It wasn't until that moment when you saw those kids with their jerseys on that it really hit you, it really touched your heart," Smith recalled later. "That's what he was about."

The family headed back to the home on Lincoln Street. Pat had to check on plans for the day's next event, a barbecue at the baseball field to continue the celebration of Merl's life. The pelting rain had stopped, giving way to broad sunshine that filled the horizon. The sun was out. The A's were setting out for a road trip the next morning.

2

A Place to Grow

OSBORNE EARL SMITH looked out the window of the plane in the summer of 1975 and saw below the neatly laid-out squares of American farmland. His flight from Los Angeles was on approach to Omaha, taking him on a journey from the West Coast to the Midwest, from urban to rural, from black to white. There was a vastness to the sea of green he saw below, separated by roads as straight as the blade of a knife. He had grown up in the Watts section of South Central Los Angeles and still stiffened with the memory of the riots there outside his apartment in the 1960s, when his mother, Marvella, lay on top of him to protect him from the bullets whizzing past. Now he was entering a world where land prevailed over buildings, where guns were used for hunting, and the only reason one lit a fire was to provide comfort or warmth. It was his first time on an airplane and one of the few times he had traveled beyond California. Smith had no concept of the nation's heartland, so his vision of the region encompassed a single word: corn.

He was making the journey because of the connection between his coach, Tom Hinkle, and a man from Iowa whom Hinkle had met the year before at a coaches' convention in St. Louis. Hinkle had told Smith that Clarinda, Iowa, was a place where he could develop as a player and that Merl Eberly was a coach who could help him. Hinkle had seen Smith's growth in his first season at Cal Poly–San Luis Obispo and had been impressed by Smith's remarkable will and willingness to work to overcome his physical limitations. Hinkle thought that if Smith was given the opportunity to play every day in a league made up of top college players, then he might have a chance to realize his dream of playing professional baseball.

Still, it was by all accounts a long shot. Smith had been overlooked at Locke High School in Los Angeles as college coaches and professional scouts focused on his more formidable teammate, Eddie Murray, a switch hitter who stood six-foot-two, with chiseled muscles and a swagger beyond his years. Murray, who was drafted in the third round after his senior year and would have an exceptional career with the Baltimore Orioles and be inducted into baseball's Hall of Fame, tried to get scouts and coaches interested in his friend, but they all took a pass when they saw Smith's slight build and weak bat. Augie Garrido, who was about to leave his small school in San Luis Obispo to coach at Cal State–Fullerton, saw Ozzie Smith play in high school. "There was a reason he didn't get a lot of notice," said Garrido, who would go on to be the winningest college baseball coach of all time. "He wasn't big enough. He was quick, he had a great arm, but threw the ball all over the place. He couldn't hit. He was weak." Yet Garrido also could see that Smith had other traits you couldn't teach, like a great attitude, a work ethic, and a commitment to the team. Barely five-foot-nine and 140 pounds, Smith had an inner confidence and a fierce desire that could only have come from escaping hardship and wanting more from life. Smith believed in himself, and he knew he could prove himself on the field. He simply needed others to believe in him as well.

His plane landed at Eppley Airfield in Omaha, and he saw a volunteer for the Clarinda A's baseball team waiting for him at the gate. They shook hands and headed to the car. They drove east, then south to Clarinda, eighty-five miles away. Smith was struck by the flatness of the land, the height of the corn, and what seemed like the endless distance between farms and small towns. It was hard for him to comprehend the gulf between the world he was about to enter, a town that by the mid-1970s had few black families, and the one he had left behind, where there essentially were no whites.

When they drove into Clarinda almost two hours later, Smith read the wooden sign that greeted them: WHERE THE WORK ETHIC STILL WORKS. They drove along Sixteenth Street to·Washington Street, then turned left to head to the dorms at Iowa Western Community College. Smith dropped off his bags, changed into his baseball clothes, and headed toward Municipal Stadium two blocks away.

The stadium had the look and feel of baseball from another era, with its wooden fences and old-fashioned press box atop the grandstand, yet it was quite an improvement on the primitive diamond that Merl's old high school coach, John Tedore, had laid out some twenty years before.

Baseball had remained as popular in Clarinda as Merl and Tedore hoped it would be, and by the time Smith arrived the people of Clarinda identified themselves with the A's as much as they had with Glenn Miller, their hometown hero, in an earlier era. They would pack the stands by the hundreds on summer nights resounding with the sounds of the game and buzz of cicadas.

When Smith walked onto the field, many of his teammates were already running, playing pepper, or taking batting practice. He saw a large man — easily four inches taller and fifty pounds heavier than the new arrival from California — with square shoulders and forearms that suggested he could do real damage with a bat. His voice, though, was measured and calm. Merl Eberly greeted him and told Smith to go out to shortstop to take some ground balls.

Eberly, even with Hinkle's recommendation, had doubts about Smith, who was small compared to most of his other players, many of whom had come from big-name Division 1 schools like Rice and the University of Southern California. "Let's see what you've got," Eberly said to him as he grabbed his fungo bat and a bucket of balls.

Smith could read Merl's face. "I know what he's thinking," Smith said. "'Give me fifteen or twenty minutes, I've seen them come, I've seen them go. I will wear him out. I will wear him out. He's only 150 pounds. He will be back on a bus or a plane.' Twenty-five or thirty minutes later, he's still out there banging them, trying to figure out how he's going to break me. Then he found out I wasn't your normal, run-of-the-mill kid. Guys like me were always told, 'You can't, you can't, you can't, you won't, you won't, you won't.'"

Merl hit a few at medium speed, and Smith handled each one with ease. Eberly, a left-handed batter, started to hit the balls harder and harder, deeper in the hole at shortstop, over the bag at second base, sometimes trying to create a bad hop. Smith didn't miss a single one. Smith knew he was blessed with exceptional hand-eye coordination, and his lateral quickness made fielding seem almost effortless. After thirty minutes in the Iowa heat and humidity, both Eberly and Smith were drenched. Finally, Smith called out to Eberly, "Coach, don't you realize you can't get one past me?"

Merl had found his everyday shortstop.

After practice, Smith headed back to his dorm room at the junior college, a small, spare space that had the feel of a military barracks. It was not exactly San Luis Obispo, which sits on the base of a mountain range to the east and is just minutes from Pacific Ocean beach to the west. He had a hot plate to warm food, mainly beans and wieners and canned ravioli, a bed, and that was about it. He didn't really care. He was here to play baseball.

Merl knew that Clarinda had a lot to offer players, things they couldn't necessarily touch or feel or spend. At the same time, he wasn't naive about the limits of the rural town's appeal to a young college man, or the potential for a black man to feel isolated in a white world. He persuaded the people in town to provide summer jobs for the players so they would have some spending money and, just as important, so their time would be filled. He had some concerns about placing Smith. Clarinda wasn't known for racial animus — in fact, its history suggested the opposite — but Merl knew that tensions existed. So it was with some wariness that he approached Bob Warren, who ran a successful construction company, and asked about placing Smith there to work on a crew for the summer. Warren was a booster of the A's program who always tried to take one or two players if he had enough work to go around.

"Merl came to Dad and me one day and said, 'I got this kid that's coming from LA and a good ballplayer, and the only problem is he's black,'" Warren's son Bill, who took over the business from his father, recalled. "'Do you have a problem hiring a black kid?' Dad said no, and it just started there. This was the first time we ever had a black person working for us," Warren said. "I thought, *He's coming from the big city. I hope this works out.* Within a week, we knew it was going to be fine. I was kind of worried about how the rest of the crew would react to it. We talked to them about it before it happened, and I got this one guy who worked for us for thirty years, Howard, and he was the one I was worried about. He could be a real redneck."

Howard Maxwell and Ozzie Smith were thrown together on a crew. Maxwell had worked construction for years, and his prospects for upward mobility were few. He tested Smith with a few small-bore insults. Smith came right back at him, and it was soon clear that there was a decided mismatch in Smith's favor. Soon Maxwell and Smith were working together fine, though Maxwell, whose nickname was "Kink" because of his kinky blond hair, used to joke that he made Ozzie ride in the back of the truck. "They were exact opposites," Warren said.

"Howard didn't graduate high school. All he had ever done was work. We had to sit down and have a talk with him. We told him you've got to watch your mouth. There is rough language on the construction site. But you could tell when they started bantering back and forth that it would be okay. Ozzie could shut him down in a second."

Ozzie found himself bonding quickly with Maxwell, a man who, he said, "was like a cartoon character. Hair all over the place. Had the look of an Einstein. And just funny."

It was hard work, pouring concrete, driving a backhoe, and running a jackhammer. The sight of Smith holding the beast of a machine as it ripped through pavement and concrete, with its incessant knifing and thunderous pounding, stays with Warren to this day. He laughed at the memory of Smith mastering the powerful tool. "It doesn't beat you," Warren said. "You beat it. You've got to hold that thing just right because it is so heavy that you either go forward, right, or left. After you lift that heavy jackhammer for an hour, you are pooped. And if you fight it, it's even worse. I know we had a few laughs the first time we put him on there." It took Ozzie a few days, but he caught on. He held the handles of the machine as it jutted up and down, and he joked that his hands and arms were still shaking at night when he was trying to play baseball. "How do you expect me to do this all day and try to hit the ball at night?" Smith said.

Smith took on all the hard work without complaint, earning about $5 an hour. The other player working for Warren Construction was Paul Desjarlais, one of his college teammates who, it turned out, didn't have Smith's work ethic, Warren said. "Work wasn't his thing. He was more into the social life." There is a picture of the two of them from that time, Desjarlais, shirtless and smiling on the front of a backhoe, looking carefree, and Smith, sitting in the cab and wearing a hat, both of them looking quite out of context.

Otherwise, Smith fit right in. He didn't have the cockiness of a lot of athletes. He was likable and gracious and hardworking, and those were attributes the people of Clarinda readily embraced.

"He let a lot of people get close to him," Warren said. "So other people let him get close to them." Warren said Smith's intelligence was obvious, and he was easy to talk to about any number of subjects. "He talked about what he had at home. We knew his family wasn't wealthy. He talked about how poor they were and how he got his speed by throwing the baseball over the roof and running to the other side to catch it."

Smith said that the summer in Clarinda taught him responsibility, how to live on his own, pay bills, make decisions on his own. "So I grew as an adult and from the goodness of people," Smith said. "Coming to a situation like this as an African American kid and watching how open people were to me becoming part of the community and how they opened their arms taught me that there were some good people in the world, that, given the environment I had come from, it is not that harsh everywhere you go."

Smith wanted to share some portion of that experience with his mother, Marvella, back in Los Angeles. The summer had given him his first taste of fresh Iowa sweet corn, which tastes almost like dessert. Smith was so fond of this newfound delicacy that he asked if he could ship a box of it home to his mother in California. Warren's mother was so touched by the request that she paid for the shipping and sent the corn on its way.

"It was a weird feeling at first," Smith said about living in a nearly all-white world. "Anytime you are in a situation like that, it can be uncomfortable. But knowing the Eberlys and the people here made it feel right and made me feel welcome." He embraced Clarinda, even the characters like Howard, and the town returned the affection. "It was almost like finding yourself in Mayberry," Smith said of the mythical town that served as the setting for *The Andy Griffith Show*. "People around here didn't lock their doors, and they'd leave their keys in their cars."

Warren, the owner of the construction company, made a promise to his young worker who ran the jackhammer. "If you ever make it to the big leagues and come back to the A's banquet, I will pick you up in a limo," he said.

Smith soon became a fan favorite as well. When he ran to his position at shortstop to start the game, he would do a backflip and the crowd would go wild. No other baseball player they had seen had ever done that. But when they saw how he could go after ground balls, they realized that he wasn't being showy with his gymnastics. It was all just his way of getting mentally ready. "He was this scrawny black kid," Bob Warren said. "Just looking at him, you thought, *What's all the big hype?* Until you saw him put on a glove and run. After a few days, you could see he would do just fine."

In the year Ozzie Smith arrived in Clarinda, 1975, the United States was still emerging from the turbulent 1960s as blacks and women struggled to gain equal footing with white men. The year would mark the end of the Vietnam War and the start of a partnership between two young computer wizards, Bill Gates and Paul Allen, who called their venture "Micro-Soft." Steven Tyler was leading a newly popular band, Aerosmith, which competed with Black Sabbath for rankings on *Billboard* magazine's famous charts. The most popular movies were epic dramas, *Jaws* and *Towering Inferno*, and there was a lamentable rise in the popularity of double-knit polyester clothing. The country was entering a recession, with almost one in ten Americans out of work. Gasoline was 44¢ a gallon. Late in the year, in Cypress, California, Tiger Woods was born. And a governor from Georgia, Jimmy Carter, started coming to Iowa in a long-shot campaign for president.

None of the nation's cultural crosscurrents had particular resonance in Clarinda, a deeply conservative place that organized parades and July Fourth fireworks, not riots and protests. That summer the focus was on baseball and Municipal Stadium, where Merl was building one of the best summer teams in the country. Ozzie Smith was only one of the vital components. Merl's time networking with college coaches at their annual convention had paid off. Players from previous years had gone back to their schools with praise for him and the whole Clarinda experience. Coaches felt good about sending their players to Clarinda, with Merl acting as their surrogate.

It was a long road from Clarinda to Hutchinson, Kansas, and the A's were almost forced to bond as a team. In addition to Ozzie Smith, there was Danny Gans, a smooth-fielding second baseman who was a strong hitter. Gans had other gifts as well. He made the long rides on the "Blue Goose," the team bus, go much quicker with his spot-on impersonations of famous people. He could sing too, and he and Smith would dance in the aisle doing their best rendition of Diana Ross and the Supremes. Another member of the team was Bob Cerv Jr., who looked the part of a big leaguer. He was strong and quick and could hit with power, much like his father, Bob Cerv Sr., who had spent a decade in the majors and lived with Yankee teammates Mickey Mantle and Roger Maris during the 1961 season, when those two had their magnificent chase of Babe Ruth's single-season home run record. Gary Thweatt, a rocket-fast player on a scholarship at the University of Oklahoma, ran the outfield, and Terry Unruh from Oral Roberts University shared time on the mound with Scotty Kurtz, the durable left-hander and local favorite.

Some of the players who arrived from California and Texas that year, just as the disco era was dawning, wore flared pants, loud shirts, and long hair — until, that is, they played for Merl. He had a test for hair length. If a player's hat fell off while he was running the bases, it meant the hat wasn't snug because the hair was too long. If a player wasn't sure if his hair was too long, Merl had an easy answer. He sent him to the local barber, who already had Merl's specifications. The proposition was simple:

if you don't cut your hair, you don't play. Players also had to be cleanshaven, and Merl had a test for beards too. He would swipe it with a credit card, and if it made the wrong sound, Merl sent his player for a razor. Merl didn't like his players drinking either, though he knew that some of them would sneak out to have a few beers. They had just better hope Merl didn't catch them. He also wanted his players to go to church, so they were offered a free Sunday breakfast if they went to services.

Not everyone heeded his commands. Bill Young, a strongly built third baseman, griped for several weeks about a lack of playing time and questioned just how much Merl knew about baseball. He was feeling the pressure of the competition and seeing the limits of his talent. When he challenged Merl, one of the Eberly daughters ran to the concession stand to alert Pat. "Come quick, Dad's going to get killed." Pat went to the bleachers and saw her forty-one-year-old husband squaring off with a twenty-year-old player.

Merl had listened to the last criticism he was going to take from this kid. Merl told Young to meet him under the bleachers at Municipal Stadium. When he showed up, Merl looked him dead in the eye and said, "You want a piece of me? You haven't stopped complaining. If you are so tough, let's see what you've got."

It was the kind of physical challenge that had marked Merl's life. He had hoped that his fighting days were over, but this player simply had to be confronted. At the same time, he himself had lost control. He was squaring off with a player. If a fight ensued, the stakes were great. Would any coach send a player to a team where the coach couldn't keep his composure or handle the athletes? Would Young's family bring charges? It was all in the balance as Merl waited for an answer, taking the chance that he would forever after be cast as a man who had never lost his capacity for rage.

Young stood there, but then looked at his coach and quickly melted. Tears formed in his eyes, and he asked Merl for a second chance. Merl, whose life had been defined by second chances, readily agreed.

Merl had built this team with a grand ambition uncharacteristic of someone whose idea of travel was a long bus ride into Kansas. He wanted the A's to travel to Alaska to play the teams there, many of which were regarded as the premier summer ball teams. The setting — playing games under the midnight sun — was alluring for players, and the scouts flocked there. A team that couldn't compete against the teams in Alaska stood little chance of thriving at the NBC national tournament in Wichita. The cost was daunting, almost $20,000 — twice the amount Merl had requested to start the team, and well beyond the $12,000 budget for that year. He went to C. E. Nichols, a local optometrist, and other members of the A's board. If they wanted to help their town, he said, they needed to help the team, and this was the kind of exposure that would do both. As Merl scanned the faces of the board members, whose life stories he knew just as they knew his, he locked eyes with each one. The salesman was about to close the deal. They bought his pitch and agreed to raise the money for the trip.

"You can't get rated unless you get to the big boys," Nichols told the *Omaha World-Herald.* "Plus we didn't know what we had in terms of talent. It was the only way we could set a gauge of our program. So the feeling of the board was to send them."

It turned out that the expenses weren't quite as steep as they had feared. The host teams agreed to pay for travel and meals between Omaha and Anchorage. They were to play four games each at Anchorage, Fairbanks, and Kenai, all against teams ranked in the NBC's top ten. Merl was responsible for the twenty-five players and the batboy, his son Ryan.

They stopped in Denver, then Seattle, before arriving in Alaska. "We arrived in the middle of the night, only to find it was not dark," Merl said, "something we found hard to adjust to when trying to sleep." Commerce in Alaska was different too. The McDonald's charged 99¢ for a hamburger, not 39¢ like the McDonald's back home. The team stayed in the Gold Rush Hotel, which Merl said was a jumping joint with plenty to tempt his young college players. "We got along pretty well, but as the saying goes, what you don't know can't hurt you," Merl said. "I have to admit finding our infielder tied up and nearly nude on the elevator when the door opened in the lobby is a lot funnier today than it was then." Merl never learned what actually happened.

The players tested Merl and his rules. Some of them brought beer into the barracks where they stayed in Kenai, but Ryan, the batboy, saw it and told his father. When Merl went to check, the players denied having any beer. Eight-year-old Ryan proceeded to show Merl where the stash was being kept, thus earning the nickname "Ryan the Rat."

The A's were playing teams not only with long-standing reputations as powerhouses but with budgets of $150,000 to $200,000. The A's first opponent was the Fairbanks Goldpanners, at the time the NBC's number-one-ranked team. Merl's boys beat them three out of four, losing the last game in extra innings. Then the A's traveled to Anchorage to take on the number-three team — they won four out of five against the Anchorage Bucs. Augie Garrido, the college coach who hadn't been impressed by Smith in high school, was managing the Anchorage team that summer. Before the final game, Garrido joked with Merl at the conference at home plate: "You better let me win one or they will run me out of town." Garrido also gained a new appreciation that summer for Ozzie Smith.

In Fairbanks, the A's played in the annual "Midnight Sun" game before 7,500 fans. The A's jumped to an early lead, and most of the home team supporters had left by the seventh inning. The A's then challenged Kenai, ranked number six nationally. After enjoying the sight of a glacier on the way to Kenai, the A's stayed in a spartan army barracks there. Kenai was essentially a town carved out of wilderness, and its field was like nothing Merl had ever seen. "On the first night we arrived at the park only to see dump trucks unloading dirt at first base — I don't mean one load but several, and it just seemed to disappear. It was our first sight and experience of Tundra Turf," referring to a then-new artificial grass. "It was finally playable," Merl said, "and we won." Their pitching was depleted, though, and the A's would lose three out of five to Kenai. Still, they were the first team to travel to Alaska and leave with a winning record.

It was in one of the final games against Kenai that Merl saw in Smith the potential to be a big league shortstop. An opposing hitter smoked a liner that hit the pitcher's mound. "It's headed for center field, and we're sitting on the bench thinking, 'Well, that's the ball game,'" Merl said.

"All of a sudden, we realized that Ozzie had come up with the ball behind second base, and he's stepping on the bag to force the runner. It was an unbelievable play just getting to the ball. A ball that hits the mound like that and skips is going pretty good. But the play wasn't even close at second. How he got there, I still don't know."

After a long journey, the A's arrived home to good news. Their Alaska swing had been noticed by the folks who compiled the NBC rankings and the Clarinda A's were the new number-one team in the country. The team went to the north steps of the Page County Courthouse, where the mayor and other officials, along with their home fans, were waiting for a welcome-home ceremony. "There was little doubt in anyone's mind . . . that our program had arrived," Merl said.

"When I first heard the news, I was pleased, elated . . . all the things that are associated with being No. 1," Merl told the *Omaha World-Herald.* "Here we were, a little town in southwestern Iowa. Everybody asked where Clarinda was whenever we went anywhere. They don't anymore."

Paul Dees, president of the NBC that year, went to Clarinda after the season. He said, "Clarinda should be proud of the A's for what they did in Alaska. No other team had ever won a series from the Alaskans on their home ground. The Alaska teams hardly ever lose four or five games a month, let alone in one series with one team."

The victories continued to pile up. By late July, the A's were 51-8. The first Blue Goose, which was donated to the team the year before by a local doctor, Bill Kuehn, was churning through thousands of miles of Midwest highways, almost always with Darwin Buch at the wheel. "We've had strong teams before, players who could put the ball out of the park," Merl said. "But from the standpoint of slugging, running, fielding—the complete ballplayers—this is the strongest." As a team, they were hitting .312, while limiting their opponents to .217.

When it was time for the NBC tournament in Wichita that summer, Clarinda's prowess was no longer a secret. As Bill Hodge wrote in the *Wichita Eagle-Beacon:* "Clarinda where?

That's what people used to say about the southwest Iowa community of 6,000 when its residents would venture forth to the big towns outside their own state. No more. The Clarinda Iowa A's are rated as the nation's number one nonprofessional team."

Somehow Scotty Kurtz, now in his mid-thirties, was still throwing hard with his strong left arm, and he and Unruh from Oral Roberts led the pitching. Unruh was 11-1 in 94 innings, with 88 strikeouts and an ERA of 2.01. Kurtz was 8-0, with 79 strikeouts in 65 innings and a phenomenal ERA of 0.97. But the A's fell short of making it to the nationals: losing in the regional tournament in Eau Claire, Wisconsin, they finished the year at 60-10.

Though Smith was a great fielder, he was not even among the top five hitters on the A's that year. Nevertheless, he had developed into a more complete player. He hit with occasional power, and playing every day had brought his talent into full bloom. The summer strengthened him as a person too, and his bond with Merl and his family grew stronger by the day. Smith spent a great deal of time at the Eberlys' home, getting to know their children as well as the couple. He ate meals there—including Merl's homemade ice cream—and sat in the family room and watched television with the family. He saw in Merl traits he longed for in a male role model. Merl was strict, but kind. He showed great affection for his family and his players, and he was a great competitor. When Smith left Clarinda after the first summer, he knew he wanted to stay connected to the Eberlys, and he did.

Smith could see in some of the players from the old town team, men like Scotty Kurtz, just how Merl used baseball to establish unshakable personal connections. Kurtz thought nothing of working all day at the Lisle Corporation and then going to pitch for the A's at night. "For most of us who come here and become part of the program, Merl becomes either an extension of your father or he becomes that total father figure, that disciplinarian, that person who lays down the rules and you've got to abide by those rules, and if you don't abide by those rules, you can't be a part of this," Smith said. That discipline made players own up to their responsibilities to the team and to the town. Merl also understood that Smith had found what he was looking for — the chance to see where he stood in the world of baseball and determine whether he had a chance to be a professional. "I believed I could compete," Smith said. "It was all about getting the opportunity."

When Smith returned to Cal Poly–San Luis Obispo, he was no longer a skinny kid with some talent. He was starting to hit, he could steal bases, and his defense was peerless. Professional teams started to take notice. After his junior year, Smith was drafted by the Detroit Tigers in the eighth round. One of his first calls was to Merl, seeking his summer coach's advice. The Tigers were offering Smith an $8,500 bonus. Smith wanted $10,000. He was so close to earning his degree, and he thought he could earn at least that much in a job outside of baseball. Merl told him it wouldn't hurt to ask. The Tigers said they didn't have more to offer, and Smith turned them down. Instead, he spent another summer with Merl and the A's.

The team was building quite a reputation at that point, and Merl found that coaches were eager to talk to him about sending players to the cornfields. He now had to make hard choices about selecting players rather than worrying about having nine players who wouldn't get embarrassed, as in the early days. He and Pat made one significant change in the program that would bring the town in more as partners. The dorms at the junior college weren't really suitable for the players for an entire summer. So Pat and Merl decided that they would ask families in town to take the players in, provide them with meals and a nurturing environment, and give them a real taste of Midwestern hospitality. Pat had some trouble at first getting enough families to participate, so in the early years she and Merl hosted seven players in their basement, in addition to their five children still living at home. They believed in making room for more.

Ozzie Smith's host "mother" during his second summer was Anabel Lisle, whose family had founded the most successful business in the history of the town. Smith spent a lot of his free time, though, at the Eberlys' house. Pat recalled his penchant for sitting on the front porch and polishing his shoes. He blended in easily with the Eberly children, especially Julie and Rick, the older of the siblings. "He seemed like family," Pat said.

Danny Gans's performance on the field was even better than his impromptu impressions that made the bus trips bearable. Gans hit .391 for the year and put himself in a position to be drafted the next summer. He would play a single season in the minors for the White Sox, his career ended by a serious injury to his Achilles tendon. He would go on to become a professional using his other talents — on Broadway and as a headliner in Las Vegas, where he earned the Entertainer of the Year Award twelve times. He also had roles in movies, including one as the third baseman in the movie *Bull Durham*.

In 1976, Merl had created the toughest schedule yet for the A's — all chiefs, no Indians — and they went on to a record of 65-13. For the first time in team history, they placed third in the NBC national tournament, where Smith won the Sportsmanship Award.

Merl's son Rick Eberly, a taciturn kid who could hit like his dad in his playing prime, was positioned at third base next to Smith. Eberly was playing for the A's after his first year in junior college, and he was intimidated by the competition. He struggled at the plate — rare for a son of Merl — but he was learning more about what it took to play the game at this level by watching Smith. "His work ethic was unbelievable," Rick Eberly said. "Nobody compared to the time he would spend on his art, and that was fielding. Dad hit him one hundred a night — that was pretty regular. It carried over to some of us. We would put more time in. He was just a leader the way he did things. He wasn't a great hitter, but he would hit .300. He saved more runs than most people ever drive in."

Just four years removed from being seen as a kid with limited potential, Smith returned to California for school this time as an almost certain pro prospect. He was drafted in the fourth round by the San Diego Padres, higher than the year before, but he was offered less money because he had lost the leverage that college juniors have — namely, the prospect of choosing school over signing a professional contract.

"Being the good businessman I am, I signed for $5,000," Smith said, laughing, "and a bus ticket to Walla Walla, Washington," where he had his first minor league assignment with the Walla Walla Padres, a Single A affiliate. After only sixty-six games there, he was called up to San Diego, where he played for two years before being traded to St. Louis. He remained in the majors for the next eighteen years.

3

"Come Out or Get Out"

MERL EBERLY CROUCHED behind the aged wooden grandstand at the Clarinda High School football field and hurled insults and rocks at the players who had turned out for practice that crisp fall afternoon. He had a great arm and great aim. He was with three of his friends, and this was their idea of fun. They had become experts at wasting time. Trying more to annoy the players than to hurt them, they were clearly looking for attention, and it wasn't long before they got it. The new coach, John Tedore, a jut-jawed World War II hero and former University of Iowa quarterback, saw them out of the corner of his eye and lit out toward them in a full sprint. Merl's gutless sidekicks took off down the street as fast as they could, but Merl just stood there. Sometimes the second chance comes at a moment you least expect it.

Tedore sized him up quickly, just as he did with men in the military and on the football field. Merl had an athlete's body, six-foot-two and 190 pounds. With his ink-black hair, slicked over to the side, he was a handsome young man. He also had a pair of dark eyes that conveyed sadness. Tedore got close to him, pulled his shoulders back, thrust out his chest, and gave Merl a challenge: "Come out or get out."

Tedore, who had led men in combat, easily won over the wayward teenager. Merl had been looking for a long time for someone to see something other than no good in him. He was a high school dropout deluding himself by thinking that he and his buddies had become men because they had jobs, drank, and did pretty much as they pleased. "There were five or six of us, running around, trying to be big men," Merl said. "We were earning our money, being our own bosses. We'd come down to watch practice and mostly to pick on our friends."

They were no match for Tedore, who was a type they had only seen in the movies, a man who battled the Nazis in Italy and France. His unit, a forerunner of U.S. Army Special Forces, specialized in dangerous night raids. The black boot polish on their faces earned them the name "Black Devils" from the Nazis, and the label took hold. They were in battle almost constantly, attacking machine gun nests, conducting dangerous, tip-of-the-spear kind of raids. In a letter home to his parents, published in the *Waterloo Courier* on June 22, 1944, Tedore wrote:

> We walked and fought all the way, mostly through the mountains and at times it got pretty rough. For four days and nights, we weren't able to sleep because we had the Germans running pretty fast, and since they were doing that, I could see why we kept after them. I was glad in a way because we were able to get finished quicker. Our forces were the first troops into Rome, and I guess that will be something to be proud about.

In Tedore's unit, 400 men died and 2,000 were wounded. Tedore spent 254 days in combat, and 235 days on the front, by the end of the war. He never sustained a serious injury and earned a Bronze Star. In 2015 Tedore and other members of his unit were awarded the Congressional Gold Medal, the highest civilian award the U.S. Congress can deliver. Past recipients have included General Douglas MacArthur, the Tuskegee Airmen, and Winston Churchill.

Tedore's heroics did not stop in Italy. He returned from war to quarterback the University of Iowa Hawkeyes and was cocaptain of the baseball team. A natural leader, he chose teaching as his profession. When he arrived in Clarinda, his reputation had preceded him, giving him instant stature in the small town. He was what most folks in Clarinda would call a "man's man." He was a strict teacher in the classroom and on the football field, imposing a military-style discipline on his teams and riding his players hard. Those who didn't give full effort soon found themselves doing laps on the cinder track that encircled the field, which for some reason measured only four hundred yards around instead of the standard quarter-mile. He also didn't hesitate to punch a player in the chest or slap his helmet with an open palm, inspiring that strange blend of fear and admiration common among football coaches of that era. His players lived for his validation.

When he encountered Merl at the fence that day, Tedore could see in the teenager's face that he wanted something but didn't seem to know how to ask. He talked to another coach, Al Gray, who knew about Merl's past. Gray told him that the young man was from a broken home, his family was poor, and he was rudderless. Merl had been told by his grandparents that he would have to go back to school if he was going to live with them.

Merl was struck by the attention Tedore showed him, even if it seemed negative. Tedore was the type of man who had been absent from Merl's life, a role model who was strong and principled. So, after more than two years of being out of school, Merl decided to re-enroll. He was now behind kids with whom he had started elementary school, when his life was less filled with conflict and contradiction. He would be entering school as a sophomore while his original classmates were starting their senior year. Within a couple of days, he went to Tedore and asked for a chance to make the football team. He found it an easy sell. Tedore was sympathetic to Merl, and it didn't take long for the coach to see the athletic and human potential in the young man who had been the team's tormentor. Merl stayed in school this time, in large part because "coaches had such a big impact on me with their discipline. I liked it when I went back."

The routine of school and football practice stood in stark contrast to the life he had been living. Before his return, Merl would spend time with his friends, who were all equally unambitious and shared an uncommon ability to while away hours on end. One of their favorite pastimes was "noodling," as hand-fishing was called, on the Nodaway River. It was a primitive kind of fishing, with a limited kind of reward, but in rural Iowa and throughout the Midwest it was also something of a manhood test.

Merl would lay his lanky frame flat out along the riverbank, his strong right arm feeling for a hole where a flathead catfish might be swimming. He read the banks of the river well and knew the locations of the natural cavities formed by tree roots and rocks. If the hole was too big, there might be a beaver or some other creature inside. If a catfish was there, though, he would know soon enough by the sting of its strong bite on his hand. If he could hang tough and get ahold of the fish by latching his fingers onto the gill and mouth, he would have his catch. He thrilled to the rush of pulling it from the water. Sometimes he'd haul in one weighing forty pounds, though twenty was more the norm. It was all a matter of feel. He didn't need a line, a pole, or bait, which was good, because he couldn't afford any of it.

He often walked the mile from Clarinda to the river with his teenage friends Richard Graham and Wayne Johnson, all of them like latter-day Huck Finns. Rather than noodling themselves, Graham and Johnson more often served as lookouts, scouting up and down the river, watching for a county sheriff. Merl was the one with the physical skill and courage. When he succeeded, which was often, they would take the fish back to Clarinda, and a friend at the A&W Drive-In would fry it for them — a gourmet meal by their standards. The fact that noodling was illegal in Iowa only added to the allure.

Sometimes the three of them would walk five miles to the bridge at Shambaugh and back. They had nothing better to do. They spent time drinking, committing petty crimes like stealing melons, thinking about girls. Merl had a volcanic temper and got into more than his share of fights. World War II had ended and the Eisenhower Era had begun. While rural America was just starting to hum with smaller factories and larger farms, Merl was not enjoying the easygoing times of *American Graffiti.* His future seemed not just bleak, but blank. There were some small factory jobs in town, but most of them required a high school education. He did more menial work. His parents' divorce had driven him from Clarinda, but his parents came to realize it would ultimately be a better place for him. Returning to Clarinda was a move that may well have saved his life.

Merl James Eberly was born in a tar-paper shack just west of Clarinda on May 13, 1935, in the crush of the Depression. The price of corn had fallen in some places to just 8¢ or 10¢ a bushel. The countryside sometimes smelled like popcorn as many families put corn rather than coal in their stoves because it was cheaper. Only about one in ten farm homes in Iowa had electricity or indoor plumbing. Saturday baths, the only baths of the week, were a family ritual in preparation for Sunday church services.

Before the Depression, most people in Iowa wouldn't have thought of going on welfare. Newspapers used to publish the names of those on assistance as a form of public shaming. When faced with starving families, however, proud men signed up and took the aid. For many others, the weight of financial hardship was unbearable. There were incidents of mob violence at courthouses, with angry farmers protesting foreclosure proceedings. In LeMars, a mob dragged a judge from the bench, pummeled him, and threatened to lynch him. The civil disorder in rural Iowa was far greater than at any time in the 1960s. The depth of anger and despair among farmers could be seen throughout the state.

State officials tried to maintain some sense of normalcy, like holding the annual Iowa State Fair, which, in 1935, also held the first statewide amateur baseball tournament. And on the day Merl was born, the Senate Finance Committee in Washington, DC, approved President Franklin D. Roosevelt's proposal for a program called Social Security to help relieve poverty in old age. FDR's Works Progress Administration (WPA) and Civilian

Conservation Corps (CCC) programs were delivering some jobs and work, with an average paycheck of $6 a week, but times were still hard, particularly if you didn't grow your own food. It would take a world war to change that.

Merl's parents, Merl Andrew and Ada Mae, were simple people with complicated problems. His father worked at the Pearson Coal Mine just west of town, barely making enough money to support his family. They lived in their shack, and if they had any upward mobility, it seemed a very slow trajectory. A pleasant man and much smaller than his son, Merl Sr. was trying to make it in rural America. A lack of money presented constant struggle. He and Ada Mae fought often, and they could never reconcile their ample differences. So when Merl was four, they divorced, a rarity for couples in that time. Merl, along with his older sister, Martha, left for California with their father near the start of World War II. Merl Sr., like so many Americans, thought it was a place of prosperity and promise. But that didn't work out either, and they returned to Clarinda.

After finishing eighth grade, Merl was sent to live with his mother, who had moved to Omaha; she had also remarried and had three daughters. His mother had little money, and Merl had trouble connecting in this new family, and at times he felt like a burden to her. When he was a sophomore in high school, he developed a severe kidney ailment and was forced to drop out of school after less than a month. When he had recovered, his mother's advice was blunt: why don't you just get a job and start contributing to the support of your family?

So he did, as a teenager with limited education and few options. He managed to get a menial job with the Vess Cola plant in Omaha and was able to start bringing some money home. Most of the other workers were older and would go out drinking after a day's work. It wasn't long before Merl was going along with them, to the point that he would wake up in the morning and wonder about getting enough money to buy more booze.

It was a destructive cycle. His roots in a rough rural subculture did not help him in Omaha. He received little real guidance at home, the people with whom he worked enabled his drinking, and it seemed that each successive day was a repeat of the dreadful one that had preceded it. For a young man from small-town Iowa, Omaha represented the big city, but Merl was not ready to handle it. He had tried out for the football team before he left school, but ironically, given the size to which he would ultimately grow, he was cut for being too small. While he was visiting Clarinda the summer he was sixteen, his grandparents asked him to come back and live with them. Merl's mother agreed that he should move back to Clarinda, setting her son free before his seventeenth birthday, but perhaps knowing he would be in a better place.

Clarinda had long been a place for second chances, almost ever since the town was founded in 1853. Located twelve miles north of the Missouri border, Clarinda served as a relatively safe passageway for slaves fleeing Missouri. Some were using a "stop and start" strategy to get to Canada and stayed in Clarinda, the first town of any size they came to in free territory, only temporarily, but after the start of the Civil War in 1861, others decided to settle there and raise their families, attend the public schools, and bury their dead in the cemetery at the north edge of town. The people of Clarinda for the most part embraced the new arrivals.

Iowa was an unwavering supporter of the Union during the Civil War, and its regiments fought battles throughout the South. Page County sent 512 soldiers to the Union Army — more than 10 percent of its population — and its people were invested in the Union cause. Iowa's governor, W. M. Stone, announced that he would award a "silken banner worth $100 to the county that made the largest contribution toward the support of families of soldiers." Page County, with its county seat of Clarinda, won the contest.

The 160-acre town was platted into a clean-cut checkerboard with straight-line streets and a "public block" in the middle. A signature design feature, the block would be bracketed by 100-foot-wide, boulevard-style roads running two blocks in every direction and forming the town's rough boundaries, including Lincoln Street to the north. Clarinda grew incrementally as it added local businesses like the Hotel Clarinda, the *Clarinda Herald-Journal,* and Hawley's store, which sold everything from "needles to cook stoves and barrels of salt."

Clarinda's soil was fertile, conducive to growing wheat, oats, barley, rye, corn, and potatoes "almost without effort," according to the WPA history of Page County. There were even sandy patches, which helped in the making of cement. Iowa, the "first free child of the Missouri Compromise," was a state primed for growth, with "95 percent of its surface capable for a high state of cultivation."

The town built its own railway, and on July 4, 1872, N. C. Ridenour wrote in the *Page County Democrat:* "For the past few months our citizens have been working for a railroad almost day and night, and we are glad to announce that they have at last achieved the long-talked-of project, and on the first day of Oct. 1872, Clarinda will have railway connection with the outside world. In this work our citizens have done nobly." Clarinda would be bypassed by the larger lines, however, and thus consigned to small-town status.

Nevertheless, other growth was coming to town. In 1884 the construction of a "state hospital for the insane" was approved for the north end of town. This structure was so massive that upon its completion it would be the largest continuous government building until the Pentagon was built. The complex, which was built in an "irregular pattern that brought sunshine into every room," brought hundreds of jobs to Clarinda. The original structure, with multiple additions, would one day carry the more benign name of the Clarinda Treatment Complex.

City boosters also wanted to develop the public block and several times proposed construction of a county courthouse, only to have voters reject the issuance of bonds. The year after the hospital was approved, however, voters approved money for construction of the county courthouse and the cornerstone was laid on July 4, 1885. It had fireproof vaults to store records and was heated with steam, both rare amenities in that era. It also featured fine oil portraits of presidents like John Quincy Adams. The two-story structure, listed on the National Register of Historic Places, was topped with a clock tower 150 feet high.

Just two blocks south of the county courthouse, as a curtain of rain poured down on the morning of April 28, 1903, Theodore Roosevelt became the only president to visit Clarinda. With more than twice the town's population gathered to see their president, Roosevelt delivered a valedictory to the ethic of small-town America in a speech entitled "Now Play Hard While You Play and Do Not Play While You Work." Roosevelt's motivation for coming to Clarinda was to pay his respects to the district's congressman, William Hepburn, chairman of the powerful U.S. House Commerce Committee, whose support would be critical to Roosevelt for the construction of the Panama Canal. On this day Roosevelt was in full voice as he showered the citizens with praise that no doubt rang true to the man he really needed to please. Hepburn lived at 319 West Lincoln Street, only a few blocks from where Merl and Pat would one day live.

In Roosevelt's ode to small-town America, people were earnest and honest and neighbor helped neighbor. "Here in Iowa you have built up this great state because you had in you the stuff out of which good citizenship is made," Roosevelt said. ". . . This is what counts in the nation — two qualities, the desire to act squarely and decently, the desire to show in practical shape that you love your brother, that you will do what you can to help him and do your duty by the State — the desire to show the belief in you in morality, in honesty and in decency is not, with you, an empty form."

The president also spoke of the need to work hard and of parents' responsibility to instill a work ethic in their children. "The poorest lesson that any American can be taught is the lesson of trying merely to have a good time, of trying to shirk what is hard and unpleasant." What counts in life, Roosevelt said, is

having work to do that is worth doing, and then doing it as well as a man can. In the long run that is the greatest pleasure in life, and of all social pleasures the one which quickest turns to dust and ashes in the mouth is the love of pleasure for pleasure's own sake . . . In bringing up your children, the lesson to teach them is not how to shirk difficulties, but how to meet them and overcome them. Here in Iowa . . . you have built up the country around you, because your people have tried to do a man's work as a man's work should be done.

The president closed by giving the people of Clarinda credit for having "the type of virtue that comes to the strong man who, when he sees a wrong, wishes to go out and right it, who is glad to step down into the hurly-burly of battle, in the struggle of actual life, and does his best to bring things about as they should be brought."

Roosevelt put into sepia-toned words the folklore of small-town virtues that was just starting to take hold as many in the country were migrating to its major cities, leaving farm for factory. He was tapping into an ethos that defined Clarinda not only in the fifty years before he spoke but in all the years since.

The town's ethic was manifested in two of its more famous citizens. Miss Jessie Field, a prominent teacher in Clarinda, would be honored as the "Mother" of the 4H movement, which was dedicated to promoting good character through agricultural life. She helped the boys in town establish the Boys Corn Club and the girls the Girls Home Club. Miss Field is credited with designing the iconic clover logo, especially the addition of the fourth leaf standing for Health, to go with Head, Hand, and Heart.

As Miss Field was starting her youth club, Alton Glenn Miller was born — on March 1, 1904 — in a little green wood-frame farmhouse down the road from the Goldenrod School, where she taught. Miller would become one of the most famous bandleaders of the Swing Era, with hits such as "Chattanooga Choo-Choo" and "Tuxedo Junction." He remains Clarinda's most famous son, though the town tour now also includes a stop on Tarkio Street at the former home of Johnny Carson, the legendary host of *The Tonight Show*, who lived in Clarinda from ages two to four.

Merl's grandparents lived at 613 East Grant Street in Clarinda, less than a mile from Miller's birthplace, at the edge of a neighborhood known as Guntown — named for its frequent shootings over robberies or infidelities. Merl had a bedroom on the tiny second floor of the story-and-a-half wood-frame house. The ceiling slanted so much that he had to stoop in most of the room when moving about. His bed was next to a window, and in the winter it was common for his pillow to become covered in snow because of the cracks that his grandparents could not afford to repair.

Though Clarinda was a small town, with a population that hovered around five thousand, for the better part of the twentieth century, it was also a divided one. The two primary sections were Guntown and Uptown. Guntown was where black families fleeing slavery in the South had settled — most of them having crossed over from the Missouri border twelve miles to the south — so blacks had been living in town since at least the 1860s. Nearly five hundred blacks lived in Clarinda in 1861, more than 10 percent of the population. Juanita Seeley, a white woman who lived in the neighborhood, said in a self-published memoir that Guntown's motto was: "We are rough and tough and hard to bluff. And we come from the heart of Guntown." She writes that their lives were simple: there was "very little food" and "no electricity," but a "great abundance of love. So, that is how we Guntowners survived.

"We all know big cities have their ghettos, but do you know our small cities and towns also have a Ghetto? To me, that is what the southeast side of Clarinda, Iowa was, and perhaps still is. It is mine. My Ghetto: my beloved hometown, Guntown." Of her black neighbors, Seeley said, "Color was unknown to me. We lived side-by-side, black and white. Our people were known and respected for what they were, never race. Many of the people dearest in my memory are people of color."

There are few recorded instances of racial strife in Clarinda, and the races mixed mostly without incident. The schools had been integrated since the late nineteenth century, and so was the Clarinda cemetery. Residing just a few blocks from Merl at his grandparents' house was a young black man, Vernon J. Baker, who had also come to live with relatives in Clarinda. After Baker's parents had been killed in a car accident in Wyoming, he spent two years at Father Flanagan's Boys' Home in Omaha. Then his grandfather asked him to consider living with relatives in Clarinda, and he agreed. The town opened its arms to Baker, who lived with his Aunt Elsie and thrived in both school and sports.

By 1940, blacks again made up 10 percent of Clarinda's population. Black and white children walked side by side in school and played sports together. Black children who attended Clarinda schools were often called upon by their parents to teach them to read and write. One young black woman who was the high school valedictorian said in her address to the school: "We don't want special favors. We just want a chance."

Vernon Baker got a job after graduation as a railroad porter, but he hated it. With rumblings of war, he tried to enlist, but at first the Army rejected him; "we don't have quotas for your people," a recruitment officer told him. After he was finally accepted, he went on to win the Distinguished Service Cross for Valor in battle. After a review by the military some fifty years later found systemic discrimination in the awarding of the highest decorations, medals for Baker and six other African Americans were upgraded to the Medal of Honor, and on January 13, 1997, President Bill Clinton draped the medal around his neck in a ceremony at the White House. The other awards given that day were posthumous. Baker's citation highlighted his "conspicuous gallantry and intrepidity at the risk of his own life above and beyond the call of duty in action" for his valor in battle near Viareggio, Italy, on May 6, 1945. A plaque commemorating Vernon Baker's feat sits today on the southwestern corner of the Page County courthouse square in Clarinda.

For Merl, life improved somewhat upon his return to Clarinda, but he continued to struggle. In addition to his grandparents, he would also spend time living with different aunts and uncles in town, often helping them hunt for food. One uncle gave Merl a few shotgun shells to hunt rabbits and was not pleased if the shells were wasted on misfires. Merl became an expert shot. He and his uncle would dress the rabbits, hang them in the backyard, and trade them to other folks in town for food.

It was on the athletic field that Merl found his place. He was a natural, both as a player and as a teammate. "The thing about Merl was that he was very receptive to anything we tried to do," Tedore said. "When he did come out for a sport, it was obvious he could be quite a leader. He was so gung-ho." Tedore used Merl at several positions — on the line if he needed a good blocker, or as a halfback if he wanted to throw an option pass. It took watching Merl throw a football only a few times for Tedore to realize what a potential offensive weapon he had. Merl could throw the ball almost seventy yards — much farther than the Clarinda Cardinals quarterback could.

After football season, Merl played basketball, where he excelled as a center who used his left arm to block his opponent while using his right for a hook shot that was deadly from as far away as fifteen feet. The *Clarinda Herald-Journal* described him as "Big Merl Eberly," and he was more often than not the team's leading scorer. In the spring he was on the track team, competing in the "football throw," which had replaced the javelin in Iowa high school sports. He set a school record that stood for more than a decade with a toss of 215 feet.

Then it was time for baseball, the sport that quickly became his favorite. Like many in Iowa, Merl was a fan of the Chicago Cubs, having listened to them on the radio. He had played some sandlot ball over the years, but nothing formal. His father had helped coach a town team in the 1930s, but there is no evidence that he had any role in passing the game on to his son. Clarinda High had abandoned its baseball program years before, but Tedore was determined to get one started again. He sized Merl up quickly as a catcher, with his large body, strong arm, and ability to lead. He liked the relentless way Merl played, never giving up on a play in football and running out every ball in baseball. "He was a dream player as far as I was concerned," Tedore said.

First, they had to have a field. Tedore, with Vern Woodward and Bill Bench, bought a book that showed how to lay out a diamond. They decided on an open patch of land just east of the county fairgrounds that had been used for farm demonstrations and walking cattle. Borrowing a tractor from Tony Jennings, a local gas station owner, the three men went to work. They put ninety feet between the bases and built up a pitcher's mound sixty feet, six inches from home plate. There were no outfield fences. When they finished, Clarinda had its Municipal Stadium and the national pastime could return to Clarinda High School.

Merl instantly showed his skill behind the plate and as a left-handed hitter with power. If there had been fences, Merl would have been hitting the ball over them. He started to do better in school too. Sports had focused him, and Tedore had guided him. Merl no longer looked to drinking for an escape. Now that someone had seen potential in him and had been willing to give him a chance, Merl was starting to see himself in a different light. This was an era of bobby socks, Chubby Checker, and *The Ed Sullivan Show* on television, at least for those families that could afford a TV. It was a time when many thought that what was good for General Motors was good for the country. The Soviet Union was emerging as an enemy, and there was a war in Korea. Merl's family "liked Ike."

Clarinda at that time had the trappings of other small towns, with a Woolworth's five-and-dime, a J. C. Penney department store, and two movie theaters downtown — the Rialto, where you could watch two motion pictures for a dime on Saturday afternoon, and the Clarinda Theater, where *The Glenn Miller Story* premiered with Jimmy Stewart in attendance. Kids went skating at Grimes Rollerdome. They ate ice cream at the Frosty Shoppe on Sixteenth and Grant or grabbed a hamburger at the Dew Drop Inn, one of many places that claimed to have invented the pressed meat sandwich. On Saturday night, folks would flock to Lottie Bailey's popcorn stand, located under the stairway that led to a dentist's office. Along with the A&W Drive-In, there were several other restaurants where kids could pass the time — when they weren't driving around with no place to go.

The high school kids met at the Cardinal Canteen, a place to dance, eat, listen to music, flirt, and fall in love. The Canteen was an especially hot spot after home football or basketball games on weekend nights. Students served on the board of the Canteen and worked at the front desk. One Friday night, it was Pat Heil's turn.

Pat was in many ways Merl's opposite. She was a joiner, a

member of clubs, an honor roll student, and the daughter of a prosperous local jeweler. Outwardly social and popular, she was an attractive cheerleader and bound for college when that wasn't common for small-town women. That night a former boyfriend kept coming up and asking if he could take her home. She repeatedly told him no, but he wouldn't relent.

This was a moment for which Merl had been waiting a long time. Remembering Pat from their grade school days, he'd had his eyes on her since he returned to Clarinda. He stood before the former boyfriend, glowered at him, and said, "She's going with me."

Pat didn't know quite what to think, though she was impressed by the gallantry. She had known Merl from sports and from classes and was struck by his good looks, but had never thought of him as a love interest. She agreed to let Merl drive her home. Merl later told her that he knew that night that she was the woman he wanted to marry. Pat wasn't thinking nearly that far ahead, but she did allow that he could call her and they would go out on a date.

Though Merl was a year older, Pat was ahead of him in school because of the time he had lost when he dropped out. They were not a match in other ways as well. Pat's parents were concerned about their future because of the differences in their backgrounds and wondered if those differences could be reconciled if the relationship became serious. Pat was an only child who had served as both daughter and "son" to her father, who exposed her to sports along with dance and piano recitals. She would be forever grateful that her dad had introduced her to the joys of baseball.

They dated the rest of Pat's senior year. Then she said her

good-byes to Merl in the late summer of 1954 and headed off that fall to Iowa State University in Ames to study home economics. He went back to Clarinda High School.

At school, just weeks into her first semester, Pat realized that she was pregnant. She was startled, and a little afraid. She called her parents and arranged to come home. She then contacted Merl, who was home for lunch, to tell him the news. "That's it, we're getting married," he said with a certitude that didn't square with the difficult road ahead. Merl's father had moved back to Clarinda to work as a mason and carpenter for a local builder. He thought his son's path was clear-cut: quit school, get a job, and support your family. But Pat's father strongly disagreed and said it was more important for Merl to get an education beyond high school. His view prevailed.

The wedding ceremony took place on Wednesday, October 6, 1954, with only their parents and two friends, Charlie Warner and Joanne Foster as their best man and maid of honor, in attendance — as though they could keep the marriage a secret in a small town. Merl tried to hide his wedding band the next day at football practice by putting tape over it. He didn't fool Coach Tedore.

"What did you do, Eberly?" Tedore asked. "Did you hurt your hand?"

When she looked back on that time decades later — two young kids from different sides of the tracks, thrust into a marriage by accident rather than design — Pat said, "There wasn't anybody who gave us a chance in hell of making it. Our backgrounds were so different." Six months later, Julie Kae Eberly was born. Merl and Pat created an apartment in the basement of Pat's family home, and they started their life together. Pat tried to adapt. She knew how to cook only French toast and cornmeal mush, a favorite of her grandfather. She had never done much ironing or cleaning; her mother had always done that. Merl took temporary jobs, doing some construction.

After he graduated, Merl enrolled at Clarinda Junior College on a basketball scholarship, studying education, and working nights at Kearney Company, a small toolmaker, to earn money to support the family. Pat had enrolled as well, and she also took a part-time job at the *Clarinda Herald-Journal*, writing mainly social news. After a year, though, she decided to leave school, thinking it was "more important for him to get his second year than it was for me." She took a job as a secretary to the principal at Clarinda High School, but her time there lasted just one semester. When school officials discovered she was pregnant with her second child, they dismissed her, saying they didn't employ expectant mothers.

Merl also continued to play baseball, now for the newly constituted town team, the Clarinda Merchants. Baseball had come early to Clarinda; in 1910 its team became one of six charter members of the professional MINK League, named for teams from Missouri, Iowa, Nebraska, and Kansas. That league folded after the 1913 season, only to be reborn years later, in the late twentieth century, as a collegiate league. Clarinda also had semipro-caliber town teams into the 1940s, including the one coached by Merl's father. The Depression and World War II drained both energy and talent, though, and the teams disbanded.

After John Tedore led the construction of a real baseball diamond for the high school in 1954, the idea of a new town team began to take hold. Interest in baseball was high, as the National Football League and the National Basketball Association were in their nascent phases and television was for the privileged few.

Baseball was still the game to listen to or watch in person. Fans in Iowa were divided between their love of the Chicago Cubs and the St. Louis Cardinals, and they never tired of listening to the broadcasts of Harry Caray, then the colorful Cards announcer, or Jack Brickhouse, the more boosterish voice of the Cubs, whom Caray would later replace. Other small towns in the area, all within a forty-mile radius, had teams, so there was ready-made competition and rivalry. Organizers solicited donations from local businesses, whose names would be stitched onto the backs of players' uniforms for a team they named the Clarinda Merchants. The starting catcher and cleanup hitter in the Merchants' inaugural game in May 1955 was Merl Eberly, fresh from Clarinda High School; they won their franchise opener, 9–5, over Shenandoah, their rival from eighteen miles away.

Merl, as the best player, also took a leadership role on the team. He went with Pat's father, Al Heil, to Kansas City, where the jeweler had a contact in the wholesale business, to buy uniforms. Merl stood by while Heil negotiated the price of the jerseys and pants. The price went down, but he wasn't satisfied. "I suppose you will also throw in the catcher's equipment?" he said. When the salesman balked, Heil started to walk out of the store.

Suddenly the catcher's gear was part of the deal. Merl was impressed by the experience; it taught him a lesson in both sales and persistence. Pat's father was one of many in Clarinda who gave Merl a second chance. "I don't think Merl could have prospered in a different environment," said John Lisle, whose family started the Lisle Corporation. "These small towns are pretty nurturing."

Like a lot of town teams in the Midwest, the Merchants traveled to other towns twenty to forty miles away to play, mostly on weekends. They played country hardball, without fancy equipment. Hundreds of people would come watch them play at Municipal Stadium, about the same time that the country was warming to Mickey Mantle and Willie Mays. There is no recollection among Merl's family that his father or mother ever saw him play more than a few organized games.

On the field, Merl was an outstanding player and known throughout the area for his power as a hitter and his ability as a catcher. The *Des Moines Register* noted at the time that while Eberly was a standout athlete who had been contacted by the Baltimore Orioles, he had "recently acquired a problem" — he had gotten married. Nevertheless, during one game in the summer of 1956 in nearby Stanton, Merl had a particularly good game, and that proved fortuitous. Sometimes baseball opportunity can come down to the one game where the player performs at just the right time. Watching Merl that night was Max Patkin, who gained fame performing as a clown at stadiums around the country while also serving as a bird dog scout (essentially a freelancer). Patkin called in his assessment of Merl to the Chicago White Sox.

When a White Sox representative called Merl the following February, he thought it must be a joke. Merl was rude to the caller, to the point that the caller said, "If you're not interested, we'll just forget it." The scout again mentioned the game in Stanton and Patkin, and then Merl knew this wasn't a prank. When he was offered a bonus of $1,000 — $500 up front and $500 if he finished the year — and $300 a month to play for the team's Class D franchise in Holdrege, Nebraska, he could hardly believe what he was hearing. "Pro ball called, and Pat and I thought we were going to get rich," Merl said.

The young man from Clarinda was being given a shot at the major leagues. After graduating from junior college with his teacher's certificate, he drove the five hours west, well before there was an interstate to take him there, leaving Pat and two young children behind, to chase his dream.

But because Pat's father died unexpectedly of a heart attack in May, she decided to stay behind and help her grieving mother. As it turned out, Merl was the one having trouble being alone. He and a teammate were sleeping in what was essentially an old coal bin with two twin beds and two dressers — hardly enough room to move — and he was not happy. He called Pat and said if she wouldn't come join him, then he might as well come home. "I told her she needed to come to me because I couldn't enjoy what I was doing without family," Merl said. Pat decided to be with her new husband, so she packed her car with her daughter Julie and infant son Rick and drove the 260 miles into Nebraska. Before that, she had never driven farther west than Shenandoah, only 18 miles away.

The *Clarinda Herald-Journal* took note of the trip. "Mrs. Merl Eberly and children Julie Kae and Ricky J. left early this afternoon for Holdrege, Neb., where she will join her husband for the next six weeks. Merl is playing with the farm team of the Chicago White Sox."

Once his family had joined him, Merl was happy. He was getting paid to play baseball and had a shot at making it to the major leagues. He found out, though, that $300 a month consumed "just about everything I made" after paying rent and buying food. Holdrege was even smaller than Clarinda and was by far the smallest town with a team in the Class D Nebraska League. The infield skin at Holdrege Fairgrounds Park was described as the worst in the league because of all the sand and gravel mixed into the dirt, and there was no grass in the outfield. The team scheduled most of its games on Saturday afternoons to save on electricity and avoid competition with "shopping night" in Holdrege. "The thing I remember most was just how hot it was," Merl said. "The places most of us stayed there was just one window fan, maybe one air conditioning unit. Every day we prayed for rain but it never came. It was a small town, real laid-back, and they supported the team pretty well . . . Back then, entertainment like that is what people did."

Even in this new mix of people and players, Merl blended right in, winning over the confidence of pitchers and of his manager, Frank Parenti, who was starting his tenth year as a minor league manager and his first and last at Holdrege. Parenti was five-foot-six, a spitfire of a man who fiercely defended his players. The Sox had new grandstands that year and sold 557 advance season tickets. Local businesses sponsored promotion nights, and a popular one was to award a case of Coca-Cola to players who stole a base. The Holdrege White Sox were a running team that year.

"We drank a lot of Coke that summer," Merl said.

Merl's best friend on the team was Jim Wasem, the only other married player. Wasem was fast — ten seconds flat in the 100-yard dash — a strong hitter, and a slick-fielding third baseman. "He could flat out run," Merl said. Wasem would go on to lead the league in batting with a .366 (he says .372) average, starting the season a torrid 12-for-12. He also led the league in stolen bases, and cases of Coke were stacked to the ceiling in his apartment, which made him popular among teammates. Most of the other players were younger than Merl, who, at twenty-two, was something of an old man on the team. "All of us guys were making $300 or $350 a month, and we thought we were

millionaires," Merl said. The competition on the field in Nebraska League games "was pretty fierce, but it definitely wasn't
first-class." Neither were the accommodations. "We dressed and
showered in an old armory and wore hand-me-down uniforms."

Wasem and Merl also had in common a love of hunting and
fishing, and on the rare off days they would go out together, talking mainly about baseball and basketball. They went frog "gig-
ging" in the sandhills of Nebraska, whacking their prey with a
bat or a broomstick. Back in town they would prepare fried frog
legs; one time they invited over Parenti, a city guy from Chicago,
who thought he was eating chicken. It was the last time Parenti
would eat frog legs. Another time when they went fishing their
boat began to sink and Merl had to jump into the water. Soaked,
he rode back home in the car with Wasem in his skivvies. As it
turned out, Pat, home alone with the two kids, had locked the
door of their apartment, which was located on the second floor
above a bank. Merl was worried he would have to explain to police what he was doing, and it was also past the players' curfew.
Pat eventually let him inside.

On the field, Wasem said Merl was "a big man, a strong man
with a good strong arm, and nothing got by him." Yet, while Eberly was a great power hitter in Clarinda, Wasem said he "lacked
confidence" about hitting in the pros. Nevertheless, his catching
remained superb. Phil Groth, who grew up around Des Moines,
was one of Holdrege's best pitchers that year. The Sox had
signed him that summer in Omaha, where he had pitched for
Iowa State in the College World Series. In twelve games for the
Sox, the left-hander had a record of 9-3, with 98 strikeouts in 88
innings. Groth had studied pitching for several years and eventually was able to add several miles an hour to a fastball that
complemented what had been a major-league-caliber curveball

since high school. He didn't have expert coaching, videos, or expensive lessons. Instead, he studied still photographs of Warren Spahn, one of the finest left-handed pitchers in baseball, and worked to mimic his mechanics.

"I pitched to a lot of catchers over the years," Groth said. "I enjoyed pitching to Merl as much as anybody. He gave such a good target. When he first got to Holdrege, he said, 'Phil, you probably know a lot more about how to pitch and what to throw when. You just throw it and I will do everything I can to stop it.'" Merl gained Groth's confidence. "He was always so much in the game, and such a fun guy to be with. When he spoke you could believe in him. When he said something, that is what he was going to do."

Merl was doing well, though not hitting with the power he had shown before, when he dug in at the plate on a hot night in July. As the pitcher stared down at him, Merl fixed his eyes on the pitcher's arm slot, trying to pick up the ball as soon as possible. It came toward him, a fastball that got away.

There were so many young pitchers at this low level of the minors who could throw ninety miles an hour yet had no idea where the ball was going. The pitch smashed into Merl's right cheek, crushing his sinuses and leveling him like a knockout punch. You could hear the ball hit bone in the stands. He was bleeding and barely coherent but stumbled to first base and somehow managed to stay in the game. He came back the next inning to catch, and only when he looked up at the umpire, who saw that he was still bleeding, was he forced to leave. Parenti pleaded with him to go to the hospital, but Merl balked at the idea; he ended up going in only for a brief exam and some medications. He refused to stay because he knew it could cost him the other $500 of his bonus and his family needed the money.

That night teammates stayed with him until the sun came up, playing pinochle, so that he could stay upright and avoid blood clots.

He returned after a few days of healing and took his place behind the plate. He finished out the season hitting .281, with a home run, three doubles, and two triples. He had done well enough, especially defensively, to earn an invitation to the White Sox major league spring training in 1958 in Hollywood, Florida. Just as important to him, he received the second half of his bonus. Against big-league-caliber pitching, however, the power that had been so much of his appeal as a prospect in Clarinda continued to elude him in Florida. Merl was released before opening day.

4

Where the Work Ethic Still Works

MERL RETURNED TO Clarinda with a new level of stature and credibility. Though he played only one season, he forever would be known in town as a man who had played "pro ball." In the baseball world, he carried that credential like an Ivy League degree. It helped him get a job as a delivery man, and he and Pat started to put down roots in the place they would never want to leave. He wasn't bitter about being released by the White Sox. He'd had his shot. He still had both the desire and the talent to keep playing sports — baseball in the summer and basketball in the winter. It was as though he was trying to recapture his misspent time as a teenager. For Pat, all the hours that sports took Merl away from the family was an accommodation that she was willing to accept. Whenever possible, they just made it a family affair, kids in tow. Most of those extra hours were spent on a baseball diamond.

The Merchants joined a statewide league in 1957 and played a twelve-game schedule. With the fan base growing in Clarinda each season, the city agreed to install lights at the field in 1958.

The Merchants improved with each season. In 1959, to give the team a more professional ring, the name was changed to the Clarinda Athletics when the Clarinda Athletic Club was formed to support a basketball team and a football team. The A's ended 1959 with a 22-4 record, winning the Interstate League championship.

Merl was back in his hometown, behind the plate, where he would be for decades to come, playing hundreds of games, squatting uncounted thousands of times as a catcher. He was also consistently among the leaders in all hitting categories, and no one could match his power. Merl was joined on the team by Jim Millhone, another graduate of Clarinda High School, who had become a lawyer; Virgil Briggs, whom Merl had recruited from a nearby small town and helped to get a job; and Milan Shaw, a University of Nebraska baseball star who had come to town to teach at Clarinda High School.

"The team was just locals, and I was single," Shaw said. "Merl and Pat kind of took me under their wing. Merl was Mr. Everything. Town team football, basketball, and baseball. I was a catcher, and that was the only position I ever knew how to play. Merl was a catcher, but he could play any position, so we would have two or three ball games every Sunday."

Briggs had grown up on a farm outside of New Market, about ten miles east of Clarinda. After graduating from Gravity High School, he married his high school sweetheart and played baseball for his town team. He met Merl during a scrimmage against the Merchants, and they talked afterwards about baseball. Merl asked him if he would play for Clarinda, and Briggs said he didn't think he was good enough. Merl, who had an eye for talent, could see that Briggs could pitch and essentially play any position, so he offered the prospect of hooking Briggs up with a job. "Merl said there was going to be an opening at Lange's Dairy to haul milk, so I came over and took a job and moved to Clarinda in 1960," Briggs said. "I took to Merl right away. He was very polite and all business. When you played for Merl, there was no monkey business." When Merl yelled "Hobby Dobby" to his teammates, they knew it was time to hustle and focus, as silly as the exhortation was. "He was honest," said Briggs. "If you were doing something wrong, he was on you. I liked that. I would have trusted him with anything."

The A's would travel to St. Joseph, Missouri, eighty miles to the south, or to Offutt Air Force Base, about the same distance to the northwest into Nebraska. They played mostly on weekends, driving for hours, but playing the game they loved. Merl and Pat often turned the road trips into family jaunts, piling their children into the station wagon to go watch Dad play ball. He rarely disappointed. "We thought he was Babe Ruth," Jill said. "He was always hitting home runs."

A few of the players were good enough to be professionals, but most of them were not — or they could do one thing really well, like hit the ball a country mile. Delmar Haley, a squat, barrel-chested farm boy, was one of those guys. The most intimidating slugger in the area, he played for one of the A's opponents. His teammates used to joke that Haley was so bowlegged that "a pig could run through his legs." There were no outfield fences, so the players designed their defense to try to hold Haley to a double, no matter how far he hit it. Duane Ridnour took up shortstop in medium center field, and second baseman Jerry Jennings stood in shallow center. Merrill Heard moved from third to deep short. Jim Ossian picked a spot in deep left field where "there were the fewest cow pies." Cal Hamilton was positioned in the musk thistles in deep left center in the "unlikely event Haley sliced one," said Ossian. "Predictably, Delmar uncorked one beyond the musk thistles.

"Three perfect relays later, and he had only a 550-foot double to show for his effort."

The A's were winning, and they had the town behind them too. Baseball was good for the community and good for business. Hundreds of people would go to the game, then have a meal at a local restaurant or shop at a store. The people of Clarinda took pride in beating their small-town rivals, and the team that Merl led gave them a lot of opportunity to gloat: after he took over as the manager of the A's in 1961, they finished that year 28-8. It would be the first of thirty-six seasons that he led the team. The next year the A's won the Nodaway Valley League title with a record of 30-4. Even as he managed the team, Merl continued to be a steady presence behind the plate and secure in his spot as the cleanup hitter. The power that had eluded him in Holdrege was ever present in Clarinda — he consistently led his team in home runs.

The A's were also becoming a destination opponent for barnstorming teams. In 1964, Merl led the A's in a game against the Kansas City Monarchs. Their pitcher, Satchel Paige, perhaps the most legendary Negro League player, was introduced to the crowd of five hundred people who had come to watch the local team play against the successor to the old Negro League champions. The Monarchs jumped to an 8-0 lead, but Merl paced the comeback with four doubles and four RBIs, and the A's won, 9-8.

It wouldn't be long before many of the original team members began to get too old to play. In addition, they had families, and their wives, unlike the ever-tolerant Pat, did not want their husbands spending all of their weekends barnstorming the Midwest playing baseball. They wanted them home, helping with their children and doing chores. Merl had to be constantly on the lookout for new, and younger, talent. For her part, Pat was always thankful that her father had exposed her to sports, particularly baseball. She knew that if her marriage and family were to work, she needed to love the game too.

A good friend and former player, Jerry Hill, told Merl about a young pitcher from Oregon, Missouri, named Scotty Kurtz, a left-hander with a rising fastball and a sharp-breaking curve. He was just graduating from his high school and wanted to play in college. He was looking for good competition. Kurtz, who stood only five-foot-nine, grew up on a farm about an hour south of Clarinda. He had thick forearms, a well-muscled back, and strength that came from lifting hay bales, not barbells. He was farm-strong. With his father and older brother Mike, also a baseball player, Kurtz drove to Clarinda to meet with Merl, who agreed to give him a spot.

In his first time on the mound, against a team from Tarkio, Missouri, Kurtz struck out twenty batters, and the A's won, 2–1. "The sound the glove made when Scotty was pitching was different," John Lisle said. "There was some real heat." That night the Kurtzes went to Merl's house to grab a postgame meal before the hourlong drive back home.

On game days Kurtz would work in the fields in the morning, drive to Clarinda for a 7:30 P.M. game, then return home afterwards. He loved the game and the competition. With Kurtz, the A's started winning an even larger share of their games, and they recruited a couple more strong players. Merl then started to look beyond the local area for teams with bigger reputations. He wanted to prove that his crew from Clarinda could play with almost any other in their semipro league. In the case of the A's, the term "semipro" was misleading because the players rarely got paid and usually were given only gas money, if they were lucky.

Throwing to Merl and seeing how he called a game and ran the team, Kurtz found himself improving as a pitcher. "He loved baseball and he was good at it," Kurtz said. "As a catcher, as a manager, he wanted it done the right way. No goofin' around. Everybody had to have their hair short, their shoes shined, and Merl better not catch you loafing." *Hobby Dobby!* Crowds for A's games grew larger, and the team was the talk of the town.

Kurtz went to college in nearby Maryville, Missouri, and played baseball there. At one game a scout had come to see an opposing pitcher. He left putting in a bid for Scotty Kurtz to get drafted. In the summer of 1969, the New York Mets — the team that would become known as the "Miracle Mets" when they won the World Series that year — selected Kurtz as their fourth pick in the twentieth round.

Kurtz almost couldn't believe it. His dream had come true. He was the opposite, though, of a cocky ballplayer. He had almost every tool a pitcher could possess, yet he summed up his potential by simply saying, "They thought I could throw the double-play ball."

That summer of 1969 the war continued to rage in Vietnam, and the draft was still in effect. Kurtz was worried that he might be tapped, so he sought a spot in the National Guard to fulfill his service obligation. In 1970 the Mets assigned him to their Midwest League affiliate in Danville, Illinois, and Kurtz began his professional baseball career. Although shuttling back and forth between Illinois and his Guard unit in California wore him down, he made four appearances in his first two weeks in

Danville and in one of them struck out 13 batters. Most players are filled with doubt, as Merl was, when they get their first taste of professional baseball, and Kurtz too had wondered if he could do it. But after his initial outings, the humble man from Oregon, Missouri, said, "I thought I was on the same level" as the other pros in his league. In 41 innings, he struck out 45 batters.

Kurtz played for two weeks, then flew from Chicago to Fort Ord in California for training. He would be there for sixteen weeks. "That pretty well did my baseball career in," Kurtz said. The Mets organization wasn't so sure. Whitey Herzog, who went on to fame as the manager of the St. Louis Cardinals, was the director of the minor league operation at the time. Herzog, according to Kurtz's brother Mike, said the Mets' best right-hander was Tom Seaver, a future Hall of Famer and three-time Cy Young Award winner. The best left-hander, he said, might well be Scotty Kurtz. He was invited to spring training with the big league club, and Mike Kurtz went down to watch his brother pitch. "You could hear the ball when Tom Seaver was throwing," Mike said. The day before the Mets broke camp and headed north, Scotty Kurtz was to get his chance to throw against major league hitters in front of manager Rube Walker. It rained all that day, though, and Kurtz didn't get that chance.

He decided that he couldn't continue to juggle his National Guard duties and baseball, and he wasn't fond of the lifestyle either. Fast living wasn't for him. "I didn't have the right heart and attitude to go on and play baseball," he said. "I would have felt more regret if I hadn't tried it. I wasn't bitter. I still wanted to play some at that level. It's quite difficult. Every day it is a job, and you have to produce and stay healthy." His father disagreed, thinking his son had major league stuff, but the son was unmoved. So Kurtz asked the Mets for his release and decided to move to Clarinda, which had been good to him. It was where he met his future wife, who had been teaching in Guatemala. Kurtz went back to Merl and said he still wanted to play for the A's.

Merl helped Kurtz get a job at the Lisle Corporation, where he worked for the next four decades. He pitched nine more seasons for the A's, recording extraordinary statistics: in 1971, for instance, he had a record of 11-3 in $112\frac{1}{3}$ innings, with 200 strikeouts and an ERA of 1.44. In that same year, Merl, at age thirty-six, and using his thirty-six-inch Mickey Mantle Model Louisville Slugger, still hit .300, down from .384 in 1970 when he was the only member of the A's to play in every game.

Merl kept testing the limits of the A's to see just how good they were and who they could beat. He had gathered his team for a talk and noted, as they sprawled out on the grass, that for the most part they were only playing local teams. So they started to travel farther away, well into Kansas and even Colorado. "Why play the Indians if you can play the Chiefs?" Merl said. Piling into their cars and station wagons, players set out on the weekends for these long road trips, often leaving behind wives, children, and obligations. "Although we didn't realize it at the time, he was revealing [to] us a vision — a vision of things to come," said Allan Bench, son of Bill, who had helped lay out the original field.

Scotty Kurtz had shown Merl the value of youth and talent and what that could mean for his team. "Scotty showed Merl that the younger, prospect-caliber pitcher could make the team endure," Mike Kurtz said. "We had won something like thirty games without a loss in the old Nodaway Valley League," Merl said. "We thought we were pretty good. Then we went on a trip and played Hays, Colorado Springs, and Boulder." That was one of the A's longest road trips — six hundred miles to Boulder, Colorado, where the A's, still mostly men in their late twenties and thirties, took on the Boulder Collegians, a team of top college players. The A's faced Boulder pitcher Burt Hooton of the University of Texas, a three-time All-American who had just appeared for the Longhorns in the College World Series in Omaha. The A's were no match for Hooton, who would go on to pitch for the Cubs and the Los Angeles Dodgers. "We learned in a hurry that we weren't good enough to compete at that level," Merl said. "We didn't win a game the whole trip. When we returned 0-7, I told people here that those teams had too much for a team manned basically with area players."

If the A's were going to continue as a team and play at the most competitive level they could manage, they needed to change. Local players alone were not enough. At the same time, Merl realized, having a team was important to his town; he had seen over and over that baseball provided extraordinary opportunity, and not just for sports. He began to fashion a plan to both change and preserve the A's. Seeing a team like the Boulder Collegians gave Merl the idea that maybe Clarinda could have its own version of a team made up primarily of college players. He would step off the field and stop playing but would still manage the team. In his last season for the A's, Merl hit .353, a year that also saw Kurtz strike out 124 batters in 87 innings.

Merl had been helping to coach the baseball team at Iowa Western Community College (formerly Clarinda Junior College). That gave him initial exposure to the world of college coaches and the process of recruiting college players. One of those players, Pete Filipic, also a catcher, would help provide the bridge between the town team Merl had started and the one he was now trying to build. Merl's pitch to Filipic was simple. If

Filipic would let Merl coach him for two years and throughout the summer, Merl could prepare him to play Division 1 baseball.

Terry Bond had seen Merl do that for many others, including himself. Bond had grown up in Clarinda and was a tremendous athlete who started out in a nearby college on a football scholarship. He wasn't happy there, though, and Merl and another coach, Walt Stanton, persuaded him to transfer to Iowa Western, where he could compete in both track and baseball on a full scholarship. Bond also got to play for the A's in the summer. That was when he learned how Merl went about developing his players.

Merl ran a demanding practice. He would wait until dusk for a fly ball drill and then hit the balls above the lights so they would be as difficult to see as possible. Players had to catch three in a row. Merl ran fielding drills with the command "ground up," meaning that a player's starting position had to be with knees flexed, hips back, and glove on the ground. He taught players to run on their toes so that their eyes weren't bouncing around when they tried to follow the ball. Everyone learned how to hit to all fields and how to bunt, even the cleanup hitter. He used isometric exercises with bungee cords on the fence to help players build arm strength and had them do push-ups in a circle; Merl often put the shyest player in the middle to try to develop a sense of leadership in him. "He was the most fundamentally sound baseball person I ever knew," Bond said. "He was always more of a mentor than coach."

Merl's success with the A's and with recruiting players to Iowa Western helped form his thinking about how to transform the A's into a collegiate team. He put together an ambitious plan, including a budget for uniforms, equipment, and travel. To make it work he thought they would need $10,000; in 1973 that was a sizable amount of money, more than most houses cost in Clarinda. Merl approached C. E. Nichols, the local optometrist, and told him about the plan and its potential benefits for the community. Merl was a passionate salesman. He told Nichols that the team would draw people to the town and that on the road they would be goodwill ambassadors. Future pros would play at Municipal Stadium! Still, he thought Nichols might just laugh him out of his office, but Nichols listened intently. Sensing Merl's fire and commitment, Nichols told him that he would have an answer for him soon. To Merl's surprise, the very next day Nichols said he had pledges from other local business-people totaling the entire $10,000.

At the time, there were three principal leagues for college players—one in Alaska, one on Cape Cod, and the Jayhawk League with teams mostly in Kansas. These collegiate leagues were well established and well funded, with connections to college coaches and professional scouts. The gulf between the teams in those leagues and the one Merl wanted to start, he learned, could hardly have been greater. "Merl was ready to give it up," Nichols told the *Omaha World-Herald*. "It was financial problems more than anything else. They were scrounging, passing the hat around at games. You can imagine how much money they were getting. It wouldn't even pay for balls. So we decided to get a bunch of fellows together and put the best team on the field that we could."

Knowing the team needed a board of directors and a real business plan, Merl invited a group of Clarinda men to the living room of his home on Lincoln Street to lay out his vision for them. One of those men was Richard Graham, his old teenage running buddy who, like Merl, had made something of himself with a good job at Lisle's. Others included Monty Boswell, a local banker; Larry Bridie, who owned Weil's clothing store; Millhone, the lawyer and former A's player; and Scotty Kurtz's brother Mike. "Merl told them what he had in mind and what he needed," Mike Kurtz said. "The board was to oversee the raising of money, so he could spend more time managing the team and not soliciting for bats and balls. Merl was persuasive. He commanded the room." Boswell, who said he was earning only $500 a month at the bank at the time, was amazed that Merl had come up with the money. "He envisioned the whole thing," said Boswell.

The men agreed to form a board of directors, and Millhone drew up legal documents of incorporation. Clarinda A's baseball would be a legal entity. Boswell served as treasurer. "He could talk Eskimos into buying snowballs," Boswell said. "He knew he had you if you liked baseball. This was something for the kids and family to do. He got businesses to support it. He used every angle you could. He had a doctorate in psychology." *Hobby Dobby!*

Merl started that version of the A's with some of his old players, like Scotty Kurtz, and then recruited players from Iowa Western, Creighton University, the University of Nebraska, and Oral Roberts University. His formula worked: the A's finished the year 44-21, winning the Iowa state championship. The A's also qualified for the National Baseball Congress tournament in Wichita, a premier showcase for players, and they finished there with one win and two losses. Again, the indomitable Kurtz led the pitchers, with 140 strikeouts in 106 innings, while Noel Bogdanski, a slugging first baseman from Chicago, led the hitters with a phenomenal .451 average. Just making it to Wichita put the A's ahead of other more established programs and made them aware of Merl and his boys. The next year the A's defended their state title, finishing 47-17 and going 2-2 in Wichita. One of their players that year, Steve Macko, Merl's first recruit from Texas, would go on to sign with Merl's favorite team, the Chicago Cubs, and become the first A's player to make it to the majors.

That winter, Merl convinced the board that he needed to travel to the annual American Baseball Coaches Association convention, the largest national gathering of coaches, primarily on the college level. He said it would give him a chance to spread the word about his team, pick up information on how to make the A's program better, and build relationships with coaches. The board agreed to cover his expenses, and Walt Pritchard, a board member and manager of the local Hy-Vee grocery store, drove Merl to St. Louis, where the convention was held that year. Through his work selling advertising for the *Clarinda Herald-Journal,* Merl knew Pritchard well: Hy-Vee was one of his largest accounts at the paper. For years Merl had persuaded Pritchard to buy one or two pages of advertising a week. This would be a constant pattern for Merl — mixing his passion for and management of the A's with his real job as an ad salesman. Fortunately for him, he was good at both.

Pritchard said that Merl, with his great size and easy manner, was a natural with the other coaches. Bob Uecker, the mediocre catcher for the Milwaukee Braves who had a .200 career batting average but who became a Hall of Fame broadcaster, was the featured speaker at the convention that year. Uecker, who was known for his humor, used to joke that the best way to catch a knuckleball was to pick it up when it stopped rolling.

The big names of college coaching were there too, but few of them were familiar with Merl or Clarinda. Merl struck up a conversation with Tom Hinkle, a coach at a smaller school, Cal Poly–San Luis Obispo, and talked to him about his program.

Merl told him of his own background as a professional player, his philosophy as a coach, and the A's successes. He also sold Clarinda as a virtuous place with good values and a town that loved the game. Hinkle told Merl that he had one player he really thought could benefit from playing better competition, a kid with a great work ethic and high potential—a shortstop named Ozzie Smith.

5

Baseball Family

OZZIE SMITH MIGHT not have been the best negotiator on his first professional contract, but his rapid rise to major league baseball proved to be a windfall for Merl and the A's. He became central to the team's identity, an exemplar of the kind of player a young man could become with enough effort and drive. Being able to point to Smith made recruiting easier for Merl Eberly. At the annual convention, coaches began to be drawn to the soft-spoken man with a humble bearing who could speak their language. After Smith's rise to the majors, scouts routinely appeared in the stands at Clarinda's Municipal Stadium. This was an era in baseball that predated cell phones, laptops, and the advanced metrics of Bill James, the guru of a revolutionary, data-driven approach. In 1978 the opinion of scouts mattered.

The town was also fully supporting the team, with families signing up as house parents for the players to the point that Pat and Merl didn't always need to host them themselves. Moreover, local businesses were willing to donate money to help maintain the program. Some would give $50, and others would give $500. Merl just kept asking until he had enough money for that year's budget.

He was as relentless as a fund-raiser as he had been as a base-ball player, and he needed to be. The Clarinda A's were competing against teams with triple their budget, and a couple of them were owned by millionaires who had no problem writing big checks. Their buses had fresh glossy paint, air conditioning, and, later, stereo music. They stayed in the best hotels the towns had to offer. One coach complained that there was no motel with a swimming pool in Clarinda where he and his team could stay. Merl, by contrast, didn't concern himself with the amenities. He might return with the team on the Blue Goose at 4:00 A.M. from a trip to Hutchinson, Kansas, sleep for just a couple of hours, and then, with clipboard in hand, walk to work and make his rounds in the dual capacity of *Clarinda Herald-Journal* advertising salesman and A's chief booster. He would write articles about the games for the newspaper and mention the A's in his column, simply titled "Sports Shorts by ME." Merl was a walking journalistic conflict of interest, but that never seemed to bother anyone much.

Merl worked at the newspaper to feed his family and pay his bills, but he lived for coaching. Coaches are tribal. They have their own rituals and folkways, derivative of the military in many ways. The best coaches are a blend of teacher, salesman, and authority figure. They have to be able to deliver bad news to players who have an elevated opinion of their skills, they have to be able to manage egos, and they have to know how to motivate a player after failure. Jim Dietz, who coached at San Diego State and whose teams won more than 1,500 games, is by any measure a master coach. He was accustomed to quickly sizing up players and others in the world of baseball. From the moment he met Merl and saw his teams play at the National Baseball Congress World Series in Wichita, he knew he had found a man he could trust. There was his easy manner, his trusting eyes, and his easily detected passion for the game and for his hometown. "Merl came across as genuine the instant you were around him," Dietz said. "Merl had the slow, Midwestern way of speaking. He never raised his voice much, and when he did you paid attention.

"Sometimes you have to make judgments on people very quickly," Dietz said. "As a coach, I've always had to make judgments on people. And it's hard to do that. But the minute you met him, the minute you listened to him, you could sense — just like how animals know instinctively who is good and who is bad — Merl came off as genuine [as soon as] you were around him. A great man isn't necessarily a rich man. To me, great is that you have been successful with your family, with your conviction, you are always taking into consideration the feelings of somebody first rather than your own feelings. And that's how Merl was. To me, that's a great person."

Dietz also admired the fact that Merl took his team's weakness — its remote location and chronic underfunding — and turned it into a strength. "He tried to instill in those kids that just because you don't have a lot doesn't mean you can't succeed." Merl and the people of Clarinda, Dietz felt, "influenced young men's lives more than they will ever know." The combination of the Eberlys and the town made Clarinda an ideal place for Dietz to send players. "I wanted our players to get a chance to enjoy a small-town atmosphere. And see how other people live in the United States," he said. His players always had the same reaction when he told them where he wanted them to play that summer: where is Clarinda?

Summer ball to Dietz was more about player development than winning. "You have to teach how to win and how to lose. You do it by being consistent with your personality. The thing I liked about Merl was that he had really strict rules of behavior, like no alcohol or drugs and that people had to be responsible for their actions. If he did have a problem with a kid, he didn't have any problem sending him home." Because of his appreciation for the A's program, Dietz tried to send Merl some of his best players. One of them was a young left-handed pitcher named Buddy Black, a player with a reputation for combining high character with high skills. "Buddy is a very special person," Dietz said. "I wanted him in a good environment. I knew that Clarinda was a fair program. I told Merl I wouldn't send him anybody who couldn't help him. I did that as a favor to Bud and a favor to Merl."

In that same era of college baseball, in the late 1970s and early 1980s, Augie Garrido, who was just making his way into the ranks of Division 1 coaches, also started sending players to Clarinda. At the time he was the baseball coach at Cal State–Fullerton, a program that he would build into a national champion. Garrido had a gregarious personality and was a natural recruiter and teacher. As his teams became winners, the crowds at their games grew. One student who showed up for games wasn't quite good enough to make the team but would later prove plenty good enough to play baseball in the movies. Kevin Costner would star in *Bull Durham*, the story of a career minor leaguer never quite up to making "The Show," and *Field of Dreams*, in which an Iowa farmer listens to a mysterious voice

("If you build it, they will come"), plows under his corn, and builds a baseball field so that Shoeless Joe Jackson can come back and play the game he loved. Garrido saw what Merl had built as a nonfiction version of *Field of Dreams*.

Baseball is its own small world. The connection Merl made with Garrido in Alaska would eventually lead to Garrido sending players to Clarinda for the summer. He knew he could entrust his players to Merl. When players came back talking about their experience, he knew that Merl had built something special. "I not only listened to them talk in a positive way but also came to recognize they were becoming more mature as a result of the experience," Garrido said. "They had a better grip of being on their own, making good choices for themselves on and off the field. They were more responsible and accountable for the choices they made. They had a stronger attitude and greater respect for the game of baseball. Their work ethic grew. It seemed to me they became not only better baseball players but also better people. The environment in Clarinda, the city made up of the people, made up of the team, led by Merl, supported by everyone — he was the leader, but it took all of that to embrace and inspire the players to be better baseball players and better people. It isn't any one thing. It is a combination of all things."

At the time, coaches like Garrido counted on summer teams to help their players reach full potential. They didn't use data analytics and advanced metrics to track player statistics, and even the best schools didn't have strength coaches and nutritionists to monitor development and health. Players played baseball, and to get better they played even more. Since Merl packed the A's schedule with up to seventy games in a summer, players played essentially every day from the moment they arrived in Clarinda until their final game in August. They lived the grind of travel along the interstates and smaller highways of the Midwest, but they also learned the value of consistent play and commitment.

"Merl recruited with the endorsement of the players who played for him," Garrido said. "Players who played there came back and told coaches what a great experience they had. When my players came back and explained all that, I didn't hesitate to send my best player there. He helped the player help himself to fulfill his destiny as a player and person. Now it starts with the truth, ends up being respect, and develops a lifelong relationship. Merl was a master at that. What he did was he inspired people. He gave people hope."

Gary Pullins, the coach at Brigham Young University at the time, did most of his business with Merl by phone. Merl would call and ask if Pullins had any players who would "feel comfortable" in Clarinda. Pullins knew he had to send top prospects because otherwise their summer would be a season of frustration as they tried to compete against some of the best in college baseball. After one or two phone calls, Merl would send a summer contract for one of the BYU players, and sometimes he would simply send Pullins a blank contract. Pullins said he was sometimes reluctant to send players to Clarinda because he was afraid they couldn't compete. He took a chance on one pitcher, Matt Young, and soon realized he had made a mistake. "He was over his head, and I had made a poor assessment and sent him where he shouldn't have been yet. But Merl gave him a chance to play and treated him as well as he treated Ozzie Smith or Von Hayes."

Pullins and Merl had that level of trust in each other. Merl had a great pitch, talking up the virtues of summer in the Midwest, the "breadbasket of America," and sometimes he would send a picture of the team's bus. But then, unlike a lot of summer coaches, he would also send Pullins progress reports on his players.

Pullins finally met Merl at the coaches' convention in Miami in the late 1970s, and he found out that meeting Merl meant meeting Pat as well. "It was a duo," Pullins said. Pat gave him confidence that the players would be well cared for off the field, and he quickly found out that she ran most aspects of the team that did not involve each day's game. "She probably did 90 percent of the things off the field, 10 percent on the field," Pullins said. "I can't think of any other field coach whose wife was as involved with the community and the team and the kids as Pat. That played big with me. Merl could have been the commercial; Pat is the program."

Baseball has a fraternal quality. Guys are thrown together and told they are a team, with the hope that they actually evolve into one. Summer ball is even more challenging because players come from different schools and different parts of the country, and they know they will be together only for a couple of months. They also feel extraordinary pressure to perform. This is their chance to be discovered, especially for players who don't come from big-time baseball schools. A player might get only one or two shots at showing a scout enough to call his name in to a major league team. In summer ball, there are also no guarantees of playing time; with players having to compete with each other, jealousies can form quickly. It is an extraordinary test of a coach to have his summer players think of themselves as a team, not as independent contractors bent on putting up individual numbers. So when college coaches think they have found a good summer program, they stick with it.

Duane Banks coached at the University of Iowa — Tedore's

alma mater—for twenty-eight years. Once he met Merl, he knew he had found someone he could trust. "I just liked him because of the passion he had for the game," Banks said. "You visit with him, it just seemed like he was spitting out baseballs." Banks knew that Merl struggled to keep the A's afloat and that other programs offered more amenities and more alluring locations. But he also knew that for one of his best young pitchers, Cal Eldred, a small-town Iowa boy just like Merl once was, Clarinda was a perfect place. Merl had a way of calming pitchers with simple advice: Trust your stuff. Throw your best pitch. "He came back a better pitcher," Banks said. "He really liked Merl. He just thought Merl and Pat were 'my second parents.' That is a great tribute coming from anyone."

Merl's style was not to try to ingratiate himself with the coaches so much as to make a personal connection, like the good salesman that he was. He also knew the value of spending time with coaches—picking up the phone to catch up or having them come sit on his porch to talk baseball and life. "He told it like it is," said Bob Warn, the former coach at Indiana State, who sent twenty-nine players to the major leagues and won 1,131 games. "He did not hesitate to let you know if he disagreed. He would give you his opinion. As soon as people were with him for a small length of time, you knew you could trust him. He was hardworking. He would work on the field himself. He would break his neck to raise money to keep the program afloat."

Merl's reputation spread by word of mouth, coach to coach, player to player. This was decades before people routinely sent emails, and Merl's aversion to computers would prove to be lifelong. He had to work at spreading the word, just as he worked at his job selling ads and writing about sports. It was about high touch, not high tech, and about following through, not over-promising, and being true to your word.

Even before Ozzie Smith arrived, Merl had started to draw a small but loyal following of scouts to Clarinda. In those days scouts were assigned a vast territory, and they usually put thousands of miles on their cars each summer. They got paid for spotting talent, and fired for missing it. This was an era when data amounted to little more than box scores, ERAs, and batting averages. Scouts sat in stands, watched games, and took notes. Their work was more visceral than empirical.

Bill Clark was one of the first scouts to make Clarinda a regular stop. He started as a bird dog scout for the Milwaukee Braves in 1956 before finally catching on as a full-time scout for the Pirates in 1968. He was responsible for Iowa, western Kentucky, Tennessee, Missouri, Illinois, and Kansas — a vast area geographically but one that consistently had produced major league talent. In 1971 he moved to the Cincinnati Reds and made his first drive to Clarinda. He was struck by the quaint town square, marked by the historic Page County Courthouse, and the friendly people. Clark also loved Municipal Stadium and the memories of old-time baseball it evoked. Eventually, he would look forward each year to seeing Merl and Pat Eberly, just as if he were coming to visit old friends instead of arriving in Clarinda for work. "It became a stop like certain high schools and colleges," Clark said. "It doesn't take long to understand that, as a scout, this is a special place and he brought in a lot of special players."

Clark would even come back for the team's annual banquet, which was a not-so-well-disguised fund-raising opportunity for Merl. In the early years, they would have the dinner in the base-

ment of the First Christian Church, usually serving some wild
game that Merl or someone else had hunted for the occasion.
Clark was touched by the fact that Merl and Pat, along with the
people of Clarinda, so clearly cared about the players as people,
not merely as athletes. "It is special because of the acceptance
of the town and the absolute involvement of the entire Eberly
family," said Clark. At Municipal Stadium, he would always find
Pat and one of her daughters staffing the concession stand while
Merl managed, one of his sons played, a grandson or grand-
daughter served as batboy, and another grandchild was tasked
with chasing down foul balls.

In Clarinda, "the players, away from home, matured during the summer," Clark noted, "and returned willing to listen
to their coach more, willing to put in the extra hours, and I felt
like Merl gave those kids an atmosphere in which to play and
mature. Ozzie Smith is an excellent example of a kid who got
better. Ozzie Smith may never have gone to the big leagues if he
hadn't been in Clarinda, Iowa."

Even the downside to playing in Clarinda — its remoteness —
was important for player development, Clark said. "Clarinda
is what you get in the lower minor leagues. You ride the Blue
Goose, it breaks down, like minor league buses. For a lot of college kids, it is positively negative. They decide: 'I don't want to
do that for a living.' And others say, 'Boy, this is what I want to
do.' And it testifies to their desire to improve."

When Dietz told Buddy Black that he wanted him to play for
Merl, Black's first response was to get out a map. He had grown
up in the Pacific Northwest and had never ventured from the
West Coast. Black thought it would be an adventure. He had
never seen a small Midwestern town or a large farm. "One night
we went to a legitimate farm and had an old-fashioned meal,"

Black said of a spread of different meats, potatoes, fresh vegetables, and dessert. "It was one of the best I have ever had in my life. This family raised cows, pigs, chicken, corn, there was high humidity, chiggers, and I was sweating like never before."

Black was impressed by Merl's imposing physical presence but also by his even manner. "He had a presence to him that you could feel. He was a man of high character and integrity, and he had a soft spot for players. He loved all of us. You could just tell. He would talk to us about life and about baseball. He would talk about things going on in the country and talk about giving back to the community and giving back to society." Although Merl ran a program driven by rules — short hair, shaved face, shined shoes — "you didn't feel oppressed," Black said. "He gave you some rope. But if you stepped outside too much, he called you out. Like a good coach, he did it privately, man to man."

Merl's need to be mindful of his players off the field presented another layer of challenge. In 1977 he once received an early morning phone call from neighbors complaining about too much noise coming from a trailer owned by two young women, who apparently were doing some unofficial "hosting" of players. At about 2:00 A.M., Merl called the trailer and told the girls to knock off the noise and tell his players that he would be there at 7:00 A.M. and he had better not find them there. As announced, he knocked on the trailer door at the appointed hour, and the girls assured him that the players were gone. Merl wasn't convinced and asked if he could look around inside. He found his players hiding in the bedroom. Merl told them to go back to their host families, pack their belongings, and head home.

There were no such issues with Bud Black, who had the demeanor of a professional even as a young college player. For him, the experience in Clarinda taught him much about the life of a professional player in the minor leagues, from the long bus rides to sleeping four to a room in small motels. "You learned how the bonds of a team were formed. It was my first step in being ready to play professional baseball," Black said.

Black also learned the value of hard work off the field. His summer job was sweeping the floor at the NSK ball bearing factory on the northeast edge of town — "the lowest man on the totem pole." He would work his eight-hour shift, then head to the ball field. This was not a make-work arrangement. If you were working in Clarinda, you worked, because if you didn't, there was always someone willing to take the job.

Black enjoyed his first summer there so much that he went back for a second summer, after his junior year, when his stock as a professional prospect was at its peak and exposure was most important. He could easily have gone to play in Alaska or in the Cape Cod League. "It was where I wanted to play," he said. Even though Black was headed to a big-time program at San Diego State, he found the competition in the Jayhawk League plenty challenging, facing players he would see years later in the major leagues. Even staying on the A's roster wasn't a given. "I had to pitch well to keep my spot," Black said. "Guys got sent home."

Sometimes it was the player himself who came to the realization that he wasn't ready for competition at this level. During Black's second summer in Clarinda, another player from the West Coast arrived, a lean, lanky first baseman who played at St. Mary's, a small Division 1 school in California. His name was Von Hayes.

Hayes was a two-sport athlete in high school, playing basketball and baseball. He grew late, four inches in his freshman year of college, and was still growing into his body. He was a left-handed hitter with a great swing who could drive the ball thanks to the newfound leverage that his height brought him. When his coach first broached the idea of living in Iowa for the summer, Hayes's mother was strongly opposed. He had never been away from home for a substantial amount of time, and she knew nothing about the Eberlys. Hayes eventually persuaded her that he needed to do this to see if he could take the next step in baseball — to the professional level. "This was my foot in the door, to see what it was all about," Hayes said. Merl sent him his plane ticket — which was permitted by NCAA rules — and Hayes set out for Clarinda.

He arrived to find his host family out of town, and he was definitely out of sorts. Pat ended up placing him with another family, and that worked out fine. "That's what struck me — that somebody would open their home, the lodging, food, expenses, getting you to the ballpark and back, doing all those things for you and not expecting anything in return. I didn't see that in California," Hayes said. It was also the first time he had seen himself idolized by fans as kids from Clarinda sought his autograph. And like so many of his teammates, he was drawn to Municipal Stadium. "You look off to the right and see these big silos and out in right field, corn growing everywhere. Right across the street there was the cattle auction and the pork auction and that distinctive aroma."

On the field, Hayes had even greater challenges. He saw players from the University of Southern California, San Diego State, and Nebraska, guys who were older, bigger, stronger, and better. The player ahead of him at first base, Tony Camara, a six-foot-five, 205-pound slugger who was dominating in the season's first week, would eventually sign with the Detroit Tigers. "I could see that I wasn't going to get much playing time,"

Hayes said. The A's set out on a road trip, and Hayes was one of only two players Merl left behind. He did get to play later in a non–Jayhawk League game and hit a home run, but he knew he was overmatched. He went to Merl the next day and asked if he could go home, just two weeks into the season. So Merl gave him a return plane ticket, and Hayes went back to Stockton, California. "That was one of the biggest wake-up calls I had in baseball," Hayes said. "I felt a huge obligation, and I made it my goal the next year to put up good enough numbers in college to come back and play here and give them a little return on their investment," Hayes said. Merl wasn't so sure. If a kid was only willing to stick it out for two weeks, that didn't sound like a player who could last a season.

The next year Hayes called Merl on the phone. Merl cupped his hand over the receiver and whispered to Pat, "It's that Hayes kid," thinking he needed to find some way to get him off the phone. Instead, the more Hayes talked the more Merl could sense his desire, so he invited him back. It helped that Pat glared at Merl and told him that if he had made a commitment to have Hayes back, then there was no other answer than yes.

Hayes had been developing rapidly. He put up outstanding numbers that year, and was drafted in the seventh round by the Cleveland Indians. They offered him $10,000 to sign, but Hayes's father wanted him to hold out for $40,000. "It didn't take long for the door to close," Hayes said. Hayes didn't bother to call his scout and tell him about the decision. His call went to Merl, and he asked if he could come out and play for him.

Merl was a man Hayes wanted to impress. "If you looked up 'country boy' in the dictionary, that's the kind of man you would see," Hayes said. "He was a big, tall, strapping, strong, stern individual, kind of like a cross between John Wayne and Andy Griffith." He was a man of simple rules, and one of them in baseball really hit home with Hayes. "Ninety feet," Merl said. "Give me that ninety feet. Run hard to first base every time."

Even when Hayes was playing in packed stadiums years later, if he ever neglected to run flat out to first, Merl would "always be the first person I would think of, that I let him down."

A short time into the summer season, Merl got a call from Rod Dedeaux, the USC coach, asking if he could use Hayes for a U.S. All-Star team to play in Japan. Hayes again doubted his ability and asked Merl what he should do. "He said, 'Why don't you go? Worst-case scenario is a free trip to Hawaii,'" where the team was training. He starred in Japan, and the Indians came calling again, sweetening the bonus offer. Hayes again turned it down. The A's were going to the NBC tournament in Wichita, and Hayes felt like he had to fulfill his obligation to Merl. He joined the team in time for the preliminary round in the state championship and started to show that he had become a top collegiate hitter.

The Indians sent Bob Quinn, the head of scouting, to watch Hayes in a doubleheader. He went 9-for-10 with three home runs. They met the next morning at the Truck Haven Café, which boasted the "Best Cinnamon Rolls in the World," and Quinn offered Hayes a much better contract and a slot with a Double A team. Hayes again said no — he wanted to go with the A's to Wichita. Quinn leaned on him, telling Hayes that if he didn't do well in the national tournament, his value would go down, and so would the Indians' offer. Hayes had a tremendous tournament, and the offer stood. Merl had been his unofficial agent in the process, laying out Hayes's options in his measured, objective way. He never prodded Hayes to stick with the A's that summer, knowing that Hayes had a shot at the pros. "He was always respectful of that," Hayes said.

With Hayes in the lineup, the A's finished fourth in Wichita, and the player who only a year before thought he couldn't cut it in Clarinda finished with a batting average of .511, including hitting .900 in front of the scouts and crowds in Wichita. He gave Merl a lot of the credit for both motivating him and standing by him. He would come to find that he needed Merl even more when his playing days had ended.

Merl was so happy for Hayes, the kid he almost didn't ask to come back to Clarinda. But Hayes was not the only player who had to beg Merl for a chance. A cocky catcher from California, Darrell Miller, called Merl in the spring of 1978, at the suggestion of his coach at Cal Poly–Pomona, to ask for a spot. Merl politely told him that he already had recruited two Division 1 catchers, including one who was likely to be drafted by the pros. Sorry, Merl said, but we are all set. "You are really going to regret this," Miller said with the confidence that only youth allows. "If you saw me play you would want me on the team." Miller would not relent. "I begged and begged," he said. The two finally agreed that if Miller would pay for his own plane ticket to Iowa, Merl would give him a tryout. If Miller made the team, the A's would reimburse him for the travel.

So Miller boarded a plane and headed to the Midwest. His father was in the military, and his family had moved a lot during his childhood. The Midwest wasn't totally unfamiliar to him because his family had lived several years at Offutt Air Force Base in Omaha, where Merl and the A's had played in the days of town team baseball.

When Miller arrived, he proved as good as his word and did

well during the first week. Then he caught a tremendous break. Merl's first-choice catcher was indeed a great prospect and was taken in a much earlier round of the draft than he had anticipated. When the young man signed immediately, a spot had opened up for Miller.

Merl's risk had paid off, and in the first few games Miller hit two home runs and two doubles. In the early going, though, it seemed to him that he could do nothing right as a catcher as far as Merl was concerned. Miller liked Clarinda. He found its people welcoming, and as one of the few blacks in town, he stood out on the A's team. But when it came to his coach, that was another matter. Merl rode him like no coach had before. It was as though he couldn't do anything right. "He was on me like stink on manure," Miller said. "He was on me all the time. He picked me apart." It got so bad, Miller said, "I accused him of being a racist."

He quickly realized, though, that Merl was just as hard on the other catcher, who was white. He also came to understand that Merl saw the same potential in him that he saw in himself. Merl considered it his job to help Miller grow, and he also knew the catcher position better than any other. He helped Miller learn how to squat to have the best balance. He made Miller work out with a homemade catcher's mitt that had a piece of plywood covering the pocket to teach him the most important rule of catching: keep the ball in front of you by dropping and blocking the ball and keeping your hands soft. Merl spent hours on drills with Miller and was rarely satisfied, at least not outwardly. "You come to realize that the people who are hardest on you love you the most," Miller said. Merl taught Miller to have an even stronger work ethic, to own his mistakes, to measure himself not merely by his statistics from a particular game but rather by *how* he played. That meant knowing how to be a leader as a catcher, ignoring pain, and holding teammates accountable.

For all of Merl's intensity, Miller was also struck by the fact that Merl did not lose his temper, didn't swear, and had an uncanny knack for seeing the good in people. Sure, Merl got mad, and he hated to lose, but Miller said the coach "never lost his composure. Even today I wish I could be like him," Miller said. "It was a privilege to be in his presence."

Miller blended in well with his teammates, his California cool helping him along the way. In the dugout one night, Miller's teammates started to boast of their prowess in other sports, especially basketball. Miller looked right at them and said, "My little sister could school every single one of you." They all laughed at him. Then he told them, "My baby brother could probably school any one of you." His teammates shook their heads. More big talk from the guy from California.

Within a few years, though, they would be reading about his sister, Cheryl, when she scored 105 points during her senior year in high school en route to a career that would land her in the basketball Hall of Fame. The baby brother, Reggie, indeed could have schooled them, as he went on to star in the NBA and become a Hall of Famer as well.

Darrell was the furthest along in his athletic career and would eventually make it to the major leagues as a catcher for the California Angels. Miller credits Merl Eberly with being one of the three most important people in helping him along on his baseball journey.

In the summer of 1979, Merl's oldest son, Rick, a smooth-fielding third baseman who was an even stronger hitter, signed as a free agent with the Toronto Blue Jays. Just as he had done two decades before when he headed off himself to Holdrege, Nebraska, Merl would see his son chasing his own dream and setting off for the Blue Jays affiliate in Alberta, Canada. It was the realization of any father-and-son dream. But for the A's, Merl still had one big team goal in mind.

6

National Champions

B OB WAITE'S COACH at Indiana University, Larry Smith, was as spare with words as he was with praise. He simply called his outfielder in and told him in no uncertain terms where he would be spending his summer of 1981. Playing baseball in Clarinda, Iowa. Waite had no clue where Clarinda was; on reflection, he decided it was probably better that he didn't. He just piled his gear into his car and drove ten hours from his home in Plymouth, Michigan. When he arrived at the Clarinda city limits, his shoulders slumped. This was his vision of the middle of nowhere.

Waite had high hopes for that summer, after his junior year, when his value as a player would be at its peak and he'd have the greatest chance of being drafted by a major league team. While he had put up strong numbers at Indiana, he knew that summer ball was where scouts might see him playing against even higher-level competition. As he drove along Sixteenth Street (now Glenn Miller Avenue), he saw his dreams fading away. How could he possibly be seen by anyone in this town, which barely had stoplights? "What did I get myself into?" he muttered to himself.

He turned right onto Lincoln Street, pulled up to Merl and Pat's house, and received their signature parental greeting. He felt as if he were visiting an aunt and uncle. He met a couple of teammates, but still felt wary, wondering if he could somehow reverse this mistake. He was looking for his big opportunity, and he couldn't see it happening in such a small town.

Merl dropped him off with his host family for the summer, Jim and Carolyn Young. This was another first for Waite — living with people he had never met. The Youngs were warm and gracious and introduced their "summer son" to their children. Waite was trying to process his situation, and nothing seemed certain. "There were just a lot of questions on your mind," Waite said.

His outlook didn't improve when he drove up to Municipal Stadium for the A's first workout that summer. He was accustomed to stadiums in the Big Ten, grand facilities that were nicer than a lot of minor league parks. This field, from a distance, looked like some county fairgrounds diamond hardly fit for a high school game. When Waite walked onto the field, though, he noticed how well groomed it was, the grass cut just so, the infield dirt well raked, the mound in a perfect little hill. About twenty of his teammates had arrived, and as he watched them warm up, he started to get a different feeling. These guys, Mark Williamson, Mike Nipper, Alan Ascherl, and the others, could obviously play. After that first practice, Waite realized that he would have to fight for a spot in the lineup.

Summer ball teams are always complicated. Players come in from around the country and are expected to somehow come together even though their interests are often in conflict. They might be competing with each other for playing time or a place in the batting order. In the case of the A's that summer, there were players from California, Texas, Michigan, and many other states. Each of them had individual goals. They wanted to play baseball at the professional level, and this was a test of their ability. Merl knew that, but he also knew that he had a team goal and that somehow he had to convince his players to put their team first. It wasn't always an easy sell.

The season did not start out well. This team was not as talented as some of the recent national powerhouses that Merl had assembled. Williamson and Nipper were clearly professional prospects, as was Keith Mucha, who had hit twenty-one home runs for the A's the previous summer, but it would be a steep climb when they played Hutchinson or Liberal, teams that were stacked with top-tier Division 1 talent.

One night Hutchinson was pounding the A's at a game in Clarinda, beating the home team so bad that Merl didn't really want to waste another pitcher. Dave Snow, the cocky manager of the Broncos and a college coach from Long Beach State in California, had been complaining loudly all night about the field, the town, and the poor state of the A's program. Snow's star first baseman, Eric Hargrove, who played at Stanford, stepped to the plate and Mike Humphry, a freshman pitcher, was on the mound for the A's. Humphry plunked Hargrove, unintentionally, and Snow started railing about "Podunk" this and "rinky-dink" that. Finally, it was more than Merl could take. Snow was indicting his hometown, his neighbors, and all the people who worked so hard to make the A's the quality program it had become. Merl thought that Snow, with his big job as a coach, might be looking down on the summer coach from Clarinda.

Merl for years had tried to repress his anger. He had been in too many fights in his life. Still, the sight of Snow mocking him, his team, and his town set Merl off. He stormed toward Snow, towering over him, menacing and intimidating. How tough are you now, Snow? Merl grabbed Snow in a headlock and soon had him on the ground. Within seconds, his A's, with their blue uniforms and red trim, were punching out any Hutchinson player they could find. "That's when you knew he was behind you 100 percent," said Ascherl, the catcher who, with mask on, head-butted several Hutchinson players. There was a lot of blood, and more than twenty minutes passed before the police arrived. Snow was just happy that Merl didn't rearrange his face.

After the game, Merl was not happy with his team, despite his own substantial role in triggering the trouble. He told them they had lost control of the game and that was why the fight had broken out. Even though it was past eleven that night, he ordered the A's to do seventeen laps, one for each run by which they had lost the game.

It was one of three brawls that year. In another one, during a home game, Ascherl told the umpire, a Clarinda resident, to duck, and his pitcher hurled a ninety-five-mile-per-hour fast-ball past the batter's head. When the ball shattered a piece of plywood stuck in the backstop, sending an unmistakable message to the opposing hitters to not dig in, another fight ensued.

But each brawl seemed to bring this team of individual egos closer together. They learned to enjoy the long bus rides on the Blue Goose, even without air conditioning and with the frequent breakdowns that would leave them stranded for hours on a Kansas highway. Different players shared driving duties when their regular driver, Darwin Buch, was not available. Merl didn't require a chauffeur's license. You just had to know how to drive with a manual transmission. Players trusted their teammates behind the wheel. They also trusted them on the field, and the natural friction of trying to earn playing time eventually gave way to the team concept that Merl was working to instill. He didn't want players to think about individual statistics. He wanted them to be able to move a runner along with a productive out, or deliver a sacrifice bunt. The players spent time with each other at Clarinda's small restaurants. They looked for different teammates to sit with on the long bus rides. They shared motel rooms, typically four players sharing two double beds. "We had bonded," Waite said. "We had come together. We had each other's backs." His wariness of his teammates had long since faded away. Now he couldn't believe how close they all were as friends. "I was improving," Waite said. "The competition was great."

For Mucha, Merl was a calming presence, a man who "had the patience of an oyster." Merl also could help players when they were struggling. "If you were in a slump, he would try to teach you by doing something you had never done before," Mucha said. "Instead of regular batting practice, he would throw it real slow and you would have to wait and really concentrate. He would throw the pitch in a certain area and say, 'Hit this pitch there,' and he was very specific. It wasn't just bulk pitch after pitch. He wanted you to make each pitch count and be specific. It really built your confidence and took your mind off whatever problem you were having."

Merl took the players hand-fishing on the Nodaway, just as he had done as a young man, trying to teach the kids from the city a little bit about rural life. One of them, David Oliva from Los Angeles, considered himself a pretty good fisherman. "How tough could it be? You bait the hook, send it to the bottom, and wait for the big one," Oliva said. When he got to Merl's house, he was surprised to see that there were no fishing poles or tackle in sight. Merl explained that they would be using their hands to catch the fish. "I thought I was pretty tough, and I played it off like it wasn't a problem," Oliva said. But as they walked closer to the river Merl told the players that they might encounter a muskrat or some other creature that could have a sharp bite. They came to the river, where Merl stopped at a log in the middle and reached his hand into a hole, telling Oliva this was a good spot to start. "Not wanting to seem like too much of a city kid, I reached into the hole," Oliva said. "My hand hit the fish, and I think I jumped back three feet." After everyone stopped laughing, Merl reached into the hole and pulled out the fish. Merl had hooked Oliva, and the other players too, on hand-fishing.

The wins started to pile up, and Waite had long since changed his opinion of the middle of nowhere. Now he loved staying at the roadside motels and stretching his $5-a-day meal money at truck stops. The A's had again qualified for the National Baseball Congress World Series in Wichita, and the players who had arrived in Clarinda worrying about whether any scouts would see them were now nervous about playing in front of so many of them. They could see them sitting three or four rows deep behind home plate. "There were a lot of nerves," Waite said. "You wanted to do so well because you wanted to get to that next level."

The field, as usual, was stacked with high-performing teams, including two from Alaska as well as Hutchinson and Liberal from Kansas. Teams from Alaska had won the tournament eight out of the last ten years. For the A's, victory had really been a matter of just making it to Wichita.

The A's won their opening game, defeating Wellington, Kansas, 9–0, behind Jeff Peterson's strong pitching. Then they beat Seguin, Texas, 10–7, and pounded Liberal, 19–10. "After the third win, we knew we had something going," Waite said. "We were very confident and close-knit . . . and we were very superstitious. We went through the same regimen every day." In the next match, against Hutchinson, "Podunk" came up big. Mucha, who had joined the team late after summer school, hit a home run in his first at-bat. He smiled at Snow—his college coach—as he rounded the bases.

Merl's confidence was growing too. "Clarinda has as good a shot as anyone for the Friday night finals," he told the *Clarinda Herald-Journal.* "I think the extra work that we are putting in is paying off. Several practices have been centered around base stealing, pick offs and plenty of hitting and the results are showing up."

Tournament play was different for the A's, especially at the nationals. Merl wanted his players loose yet focused. He held team meetings each day to go over scouting reports and approaches to individual teams. He talked about having the right motivation for winning. Stay in the moment, he told them. Don't look ahead. As permitted under tournament rules, he had brought on former A's players—Jack Shupe, who had played in the Yankees organization and was teaching in a nearby town, and Rich Chiles, who had recently been released by the Minnesota Twins. The players, after their first two wins, started getting superstitious. On their limited per diem, they dined on chili dogs at Coney Island, two or three meals a day. They passed time bowling at the Rose Bowl. They sat around the hotel and watched the same soap opera, *General Hospital.* Merl even changed his rules and allowed guys to go swimming at the motel on a game day. Over the years, Merl and Pat had befriended Alice Steventon, the manager of the Howard Johnson's motel, and she knew Merl wouldn't let things get out of hand.

Hundreds of people from Clarinda made the trip too, many of them wearing the team's signature powder blue. They were consistently the loudest cheering section at the stadium. The A's gave them reason to cheer, knocking off Hutchinson — a team that in coming years would have Roger Clemens, Barry Bonds, Rafael Palmeiro, and Pete Incaviglia, future big league stars, on its roster — and then Liberal, followed by Kenai, Alaska. The A's won six straight games in the double elimination tournament, including three by relief pitcher Chuck Matthews, a quiet freshman right-hander from Texas Wesleyan. Then they faced Liberal again, with a chance to capture the title.

"We're still going, six down and one big one to go," Merl told his hometown paper. "It's a great feeling to be in the final game, but a different one though, to be around a bunch of guys that want to win it bad. We have several injuries right now but they are playing hurt. The hustle, the defensive plays and running we have seen is the best they played all year. Our bullpen is rested and we're going to run like crazy, hit, collide and do what we have all along."

To his players, Merl was calm and direct. He talked only about the next game, even knowing that if they won, the national title would come to Clarinda. "He concentrated on winning the first game," Mucha said. "We knew what we had done. Some of the older guys like Jack Shupe and Rich Chiles talked to us, what this would mean to Merl, and to the people of Clarinda."

Chiles, clinging to the hope that one of the scouts might see that he still had big league talent, had tried to counsel the younger players to relax. As they shagged flies that Merl hit soaring into the outfield, he noticed that his teammates were pressing, as though a scout was watching their every move. So when Chiles caught a ball, he took it and threw it into the stands over the backstop and then looked at his teammates. "You guys got tight asses," he said, laughing, and breaking some of the tension.

Merl felt like he had lived his life for this moment in the late summer of 1981. He was sharing it with his old friend Milan Shaw, who was in his first year as one of the A's coaches. The two old friends would scout the teams they were to play next, sometimes well into the early hours of the morning. Merl had stature at the tournament now, and the other coaches, scouts, and even some opposing players would seek him out to talk baseball. "People knew you everywhere you would go if you were with Merl," Mucha said. "He wasn't really treated as a celebrity, but he was well respected, and he was humble. He was proud of his family and proud of his boys, and we were all his boys." And Merl's boys were doing quite well. They now just needed to defeat the Liberal Beejays one last time to win the championship.

It was steamy and hot at Lawrence-Dumont Stadium in Wichita, Kansas, and Merl's A's were in the championship game of the National Baseball Congress tournament against the team from Liberal, Kansas, their rival and a perennial national power. There were more people in the stands than lived in the entire town of Clarinda. Major League scouts were there, and so were local television and newspaper reporters. In most years, Merl considered the team's goals met if they merely qualified for the national tournament. Now the A's were in a position to win it all. So much was riding on this game — all the dreams of those in his small Iowa town going up against the giants in college baseball, with their money and prestige. No Iowa team had ever won a national championship.

Bob Lutz, the sports columnist for the *Wichita Eagle* who had been covering the tournament since 1976 and would go on to write about it for more than three decades, was sitting in the press box near Darwin Buch, the bus driver, who doubled as the A's official scorer. "It was a very tense game and a very raucous atmosphere," Lutz said. He could tell how nervous Buch was and how much this game meant not only to the team but to the town, with its hundreds of fans sitting along the first-base line. Lutz had seen the team's iconic blue bus pulling into Lawrence-Dumont Stadium and the A's, with their blue uniforms, getting off, always ready to play. The little town had made an impression on Lutz, who said the A's were "definitely one of the power players" in the field. "You could always count on Clarinda having two or three guys on their team who would have a really good chance to make it to the majors."

The A's battled all night with Liberal and eventually tied the game 7–7 on Mucha's run-scoring single. Merl went to Matthews, again, in relief in the fourth inning, and he continued to pitch splendidly, giving up just three hits and no earned runs and taking the A's to the bottom of the eleventh, still tied 7–7. After two quick outs, Merl looked down his bench for options. He stopped at Rusty Pontious, all five foot seven inches of him, and calmly said: "It's your time."

Pontious was an utterly unlikely choice for a pinch hitter. The reserve second baseman had not had an at-bat in the entire tournament. But on another level, he made perfect sense. Pontious had played at Iowa Western Community College in Clarinda and had grown up in nearby Shenandoah. If the A's, the underdog team, were going to win this game, Merl figured, then maybe the little guy from Iowa was the right choice. Pontious, nervous, grabbed his metal bat and took his place in the batter's box.

Waite walked to the on-deck circle. He had confidence in Pontious. He was more worried about himself because if Rusty got on, it would be up to him to drive him in. "We never questioned Merl," Mucha said. "I can tell you flat out you never thought of questioning him."

Liberal pitcher Bob Gunnerson delivered the first pitch, a fastball, and Pontious seemed to relax. Coaches had always told him, *Let the game come to you,* so that was what he was thinking. He saw several more pitches and realized that he was tracking the ball well. He worked the count to 3-2.

Gunnerson, a left-hander, stared him down from the mound, started his windup, and delivered the pitch. Pontious could tell by the spin that it was an off-speed pitch low and away, but close enough to a strike to swing at. He did what Merl had told his hitters to do, as simple as it sounds: *See the ball, hit the ball.* He swung hard and could hear the sound of the metal making contact. The ball screamed down the right-field line. It was fair! Pontious, a four-sport athlete in high school, ran as hard as he could. He rounded second and saw Merl in the third-base coach's box with his arms up, signaling for Rusty to stop. He stood on second base, with a stand-up double, and a grin that seemed to span the stadium.

Waite tried to get calm, saying to himself, *Now it's my time.* Merl walked halfway from the coach's box to home plate, tapped one fist on top of the other, and smiled at Waite, calming his hitter. Waite said to himself, *I've got to get a hit, or at least get it to the outfield grass, because Rusty has some wheels.* Waite, a left-handed batter, was worried about matching up with a left-handed pitcher. Telling himself he would try to hit the ball to the opposite field, he smoked a ground ball at Liberal short-stop Greg Steen, deep into the hole. As soon as he made contact, Waite said, "I knew I had to run like I had never run before."

Pontious, with two outs, was running on contact. As he rounded third he saw that Steen was throwing to first, and he just kept on running. Mucha, watching from the dugout, said it was "like slow motion." The throw ended up in the dirt, and first baseman Mike Rubel couldn't dig it out. Waite had crossed the base and, looking to his right, saw the umpire signal that he was safe at first. Pontious scored standing up, delivering a national championship to the little town that could. "If I get thrown out, Merl would have been really mad," Pontious said. "People were telling me he actually had the stop sign up."

His teammates mobbed Pontious at home plate. Merl gave him a bear hug he will never forget. "It was amazing. We had never really won anything in my hometown. To have a stage like this, where it comes down to the last out of the game, then have your teammates there celebrating with you — it was something that has never been done in southwest Iowa. I was giddy and happy and am sure that I didn't even sleep that night."

Lutz said that no baseball people had thought Clarinda could win against the teams from Alaska or against Liberal. "That was viewed as a pretty monumental achievement," he said.

Pontious's teammates had iced-down beer and champagne in the bathtubs of their hotel rooms, and when they returned they partied until 5:00 A.M. Normally, Merl didn't condone that kind of behavior. In Clarinda, if a player misbehaved, Merl called him out and sometimes sent him home. "You could not get away with anything in this town without him finding out," Ascherl said.

"If you went out at night and broke curfew, he knew, and then you knew you were going to run laps for it." But on this night in Wichita, Merl let it go. He joined in the celebration back at the motel by immediately going to the swimming pool, stepping on the diving board, and doing a cannonball — in full uniform. Alice had hired an off-duty police officer, in case the celebration got out of hand, but the precaution proved quite unnecessary as fans and players sat in the hallways talking, waiting for that morning's *Wichita Eagle* to arrive.

Shupe, the old pro, had seen more talented Clarinda teams, but this one was special for other reasons. The A's had finished last in their division of the Jayhawk League that season and had come to the NBC World Series as a number-five seed.

"The people we had this year weren't blessed with all that much God-given talent," Shupe told *All-America Baseball News*. "But I have never seen young players who are as aggressive and hard working as these kids. We just decided we were going to go down to Wichita and win."

The next morning a weary but happy team boarded their rattling, rolling cage of a bus as a band of baseball brothers soon to be local heroes. Raymond Petty was behind the wheel for this drive home, a job he had shared with Darwin Buch for the tens of thousands of miles of transporting the A's over the years. The Blue Goose took the team 310 miles north to their summer home, where they would pack up and then return to their colleges. It was quiet as they drove onto the turnpike. Players and coaches alike were feeling ample fatigue from fifteen days of tournament play, followed by a long night of celebration. As Merl looked back at the rows, noticing that many of his sleeping players had their arms draped around their trophies, he thought about his town and how the people there would now think of themselves as a "national championship community."

"The silence on the bus was eerie but at the same time a feeling of pride came over me," Merl would write years later. "I will never forget that moment which led me to reminisce about the tourney, the season and the tough moment of saying goodbye to team members. They would no longer be my players but friends when we arrived home." By the time they reached Shenandoah, the players were signing baseballs for each other and exchanging phone numbers and addresses.

As they neared the Stanton corner on Highway 2, Merl noticed that a few cars were starting to fall in behind the bus. About five miles outside of town, Waite and his teammates heard a siren, and they thought that for some reason their luck had run out and now their trip home would be delayed. The opposite was true. It was just the start of their escort by the police and fire departments, sirens on and lights flashing. As the bus reached the last hill west of town, it was clear that the team had returned to Clarinda to the equivalent of a ticker tape parade, to honor the national title they had just won. People pridefully lined the streets and cheered. "It seems everyone has their little thing to do for the community," Merl told the *Herald-Journal*. "Coaching or bringing baseball to the community is my little thing."

"People did care," Merl wrote. "The caravan led us all around town, the square and later to the ball field. People were standing and waving in their yards as we passed, people on the square and later a good crowd at the ball field — we were overwhelmed and proud to share with the community our outstanding achievement. In a sense it belonged to them. We represented them and their town and we had won them a national championship and many were showing they were proud too."

When Merl and Pat finally made it home that night, they saw that some kids in the neighborhood had put a homemade sign in the front yard, proclaiming the national title. Merl had wanted to build something that the community could embrace, but this success was beyond even what he had hoped for. The man who had dedicated his life to providing opportunity for young men — just as John Tedore had done for him — had a moment of profound validation.

Players made lasting connections with the Eberlys and Clarinda, and with the NBC World Series win, even more elite players now wanted to come and be part of the A's. "It became a tradition," Alan Ascherl said. He had come to Clarinda from California, where he played at Pepperdine. He joked about his college coach telling him where he would be going to play that summer. "I slept through geography class," he said, clueless about Clarinda's location. All he knew was that "they needed a catcher." A left-handed-hitting catcher, just like Merl, he instantly fit in with the team. Soon after he arrived in town, his host family took him to a track meet at Clarinda High School. Several hundred people were there — including Merl and Pat — to support the high school athletes, and Ascherl was struck by their enthusiasm.

During Ascherl's first night in Clarinda, there was a tornado warning. The next day he was on the grounds crew, working on the field, and at noon the tornado siren wailed. He looked to the south and saw his first tornado. He loved it.

While he was working the fields, he also noticed an attractive young woman helping coach a Little League team. Her name was Rebecca, and they started dating that summer; after the national championship season, they were in a serious relationship. He transferred from Pepperdine to Texas Wesleyan, so that he could see her more. They decided to get married, and the guy from California didn't hesitate when his wife said she wanted to live in Clarinda. They would make their home there for more than thirty years, and their son, Austin, became a catcher for the Clarinda A's.

The NBC championship had carried a $12,000 first prize. Merl insisted that the money never be spent, but rather be saved in the event that the team dissolved and had outstanding debts. He had no problem soliciting money — he was in fact relentless at it — but he never wanted to owe anyone.

Over the years the team had to borrow against the $12,000 certificate of deposit when times were tough, but the A's kept the original winnings.

7

Merl's Rules

THE NATIONAL CHAMPIONSHIP brought instant validation for Merl as a coach and the A's as a program. By
the early 1980s, recent alums of the Clarinda A's included three
big league stars — Ozzie Smith, Von Hayes, and Buddy Black.
Each of them generously donated thousands of dollars to the
program to help Merl defray costs, and he needed the help.

A punishing recession had swept across the country, and
it was hurting the Midwest more than most places. The farm
economy was lagging, unemployment was high, as were interest rates, and President Ronald Reagan, whom Merl admired,
had not yet claimed it was "morning in America." In Iowa, the
recession caused some of the greatest financial carnage since
the Great Depression. Thousands of families were driven from
their farms, and the trend of depopulation of rural areas was ac-
celerated as people moved to cities for what they hoped would
be a more secure life. Farm foreclosures were a sad reality, and
it would be some time before the issue was addressed by Hol-

lywood movies, congressional hearings, and roiling anger and activism across rural America.

The people of Clarinda, while not immune to the harsh economy, nonetheless largely stayed put, and the population remained remarkably stable, just above five thousand people. Businesses came and went, but a core of them remained, their loyal customers perhaps even paying a slight premium so their neighbor could stay open on the town square. The Lisle Corporation was an anchor for light manufacturing and helped attract similar firms. A large Japanese company built a ball bearing plant in Clarinda, convinced that the work ethic and low-tax environment would prove profitable.

Its stability was one of many things that Merl loved about Clarinda. People there didn't just know you superficially — they knew you deeply and probably knew about your family going back at least a generation. They knew your hardships and your joys and were there for you for both. They helped you keep watch over your children, as you did for theirs. That stability was one factor that helped Merl and Pat keep their own large family so close. For Merl, baseball was often merely the vehicle to try to teach something more enduring, and that something, which he wanted his players to experience, was the sense of community that was such a binding force in his hometown.

The A's provided a counterweight to the grim times, a pleasant diversion that enabled the people of Clarinda to spend summer nights enjoying the slower, almost meditative qualities of a baseball game. Tickets for the A's were $2 (a price that would hold for thirty-two years, before rising to $3), and for the two-plus hours spent watching a game, larger concerns could wait. Players like Jeff Livin, a pitcher from Texas, wanted to provide the fans with the kind of quality baseball they had come to expect in the southwestern corner of Iowa. As a player at Southwestern University, he had just started getting interest from professional scouts, so he knew he needed to go to a summer program with formidable competition. One of those scouts, a man from Houston, had sent him a list of options. They included the obvious ones: teams in Alaska and the Cape Cod League. The other team on the list was the Clarinda A's. That list alone was a measure of just how far Merl's program had come in a relatively short time. Livin had contacted all three, and Merl was the first to reply, offering him a spot on the A's. Livin accepted, but after he arrived in Clarinda he received a letter from the Fairbanks Goldpanners, saying that they too wanted him on their roster. Even with a recent national championship, it was hard to compare the reputation of Clarinda and baseball in the Midwest with the Alaska League or the Cape Cod League. But Livin chose to honor his commitment.

When he saw Clarinda and Municipal Stadium, he later said that "it was like *Field of Dreams*. When that movie came out, all I could think about was Clarinda," Livin said. He meant that Merl's program had the same simple elegance, spare surroundings, and commitment to doing things the right way, with a real love for the game. "There were never any airs about the program," said Livin, who later coached at Angelina College in Lufkin, Texas. "It was straightforward. No bold promises. This is what it is. Merl said, 'I can't promise you this or that, but if you work hard, you will earn it.' So that is what I have tried to do in my career. Shoot straight with kids. I don't think Merl Eberly knew how to lie."

Municipal Stadium was a throwback as well. In the best days of the A's, the bleachers were packed and fans listened to a for-

Ozzie Smith played for the Clarinda A's for two summers, 1975 and 1976.
Courtesy of Pat Eberly

While in Clarinda, Ozzie Smith worked construction by day and played baseball by night.
Reprinted with permission from the Omaha World-Herald

Von Hayes left the A's during his first summer because he did not think he could compete.
Courtesy of Pat Eberly

Unless otherwise credited, photographs are reproduced courtesy of Nodaway Valley Historical Museum Archives.

After playing for the Clarinda A's, Bud Black became a star pitcher in the majors and later a big league manager.

Merl Eberly was a power-hitting catcher known for his ability to handle pitchers. *Reprinted with permission from the* Omaha World-Herald

Merl (front row, far left) as a player for the A's.

Yearbook photos of Pat and Merl Eberly. They were high school sweethearts.

John Tedore, a World War II hero,
was the coach who helped change Merl Eberly's life.
Courtesy of Pat Eberly

Bud Black, Von Hayes, and Ozzie Smith often return for the A's annual banquet.

Merl Eberly (center) persuaded business and civic leaders to support the A's.

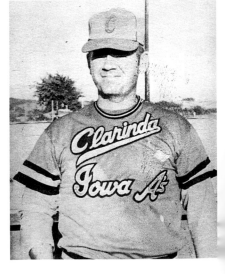

Scotty Kurtz pitched for the A's for more than a decade, well into his thirties.

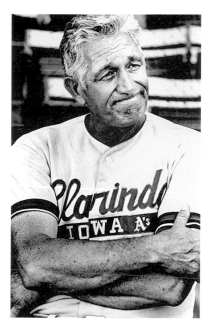

Merl didn't often yell, but players knew what this expression meant.
© Wichita Eagle

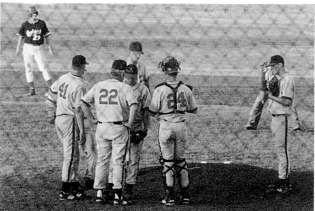

Merl conferring at the mound at Municipal Stadium in Clarinda.

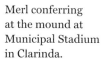

Merl and one of his coaches, Milan Shaw, at the National Baseball Congress tournament in Wichita.

The A's celebrate their National Baseball Congress championship in 1981.

Merl at Municipal Stadium in Clarinda.

Merl's view from the dugout.

Merl Eberly in the 1980s, flanked by his sons. From left: Rod, Ryan, and Rick.
© *Gaines DuVall Sports Portraits, Cave Creek, Arizona*

Merl and Pat Eberly with Ozzie Smith and Chuck Knoblauch.
Courtesy of Pat Eberly

When Ozzie Smith was inducted into baseball's Hall of Fame, he had front-row seats reserved for Merl and Pat.
Courtesy of Pat Eberly

In the summer of 2008, a fire destroyed the team
bus, the Blue Goose, but no players were injured.
© *Michael Ghutzman*

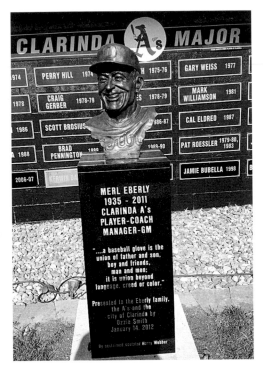

Ozzie Smith commissioned this bronze
bust of Merl, which is on display at
Municipal Stadium.

Photo © Michael Tackett / Sculpture © Harry Weber

Ozzie and Pat.
© *Michael Tackett*

mer radio personality announce the lineups and implore people to visit the concession stand, a source of traditional ballpark food, like "Merl's hand-dipped hot dogs," as well as a source of revenue. Some fans brought their lawn chairs and sat alongside the chain-link fence along the third-base line.

Livin feared the competition when he got to Clarinda. He told his host family, Charlie and Connie Richardson, that he was essentially a "walk-on" and wasn't sure he could even make the team. Merl had recruited several All-American-caliber players from big-name schools. But Livin soon proved that he belonged among them. He had a pitcher's lanky frame and a show-no-emotion demeanor on the mound. For that summer, he was living the life of a professional, off on his own, isolated, growing as a man. When things weren't going well, he would go to the Eberlys' unpretentious frame house on Lincoln Street and find refuge. The concrete front porch was wide and welcoming, with soft and comfortable couches and chairs that had endured years of use. And Pat always seemed to be cooking something, so there was a good chance that he could also get something to eat, even with all the mouths she had to feed on a daily basis. "If you went over to talk to Pat or Merl, by the time they were done hugging you or feeding you, you felt better," he said.

The Richardsons embraced him as well. They frequently loaned him their pickup truck to drive to and from the baseball games. One night Livin asked Charlie Richardson whether he knew all these people, or "did everyone in this town wave at everyone else?" In Clarinda, people didn't just know your name, they knew who you were by what you drove.

Merl and Pat did this all while raising three boys and three girls on one paycheck that Merl earned from the Clarinda newspaper. When they were growing up, the Eberly children didn't realize how tight the money was, but they didn't crave a lot in the way of possessions. Joy Eberly said the family may have been poor, "but we didn't know it." Merl used to keep a "shoe list" in his wallet, showing which child was next in line for a new pair when they could afford it. He kept a dime jar in the front window and saved all year for money for vacation. Rick Eberly described his family as "tweeners": they straddled the upper-middle class that Pat's family had represented and the more working class of Merl's clan. The kids felt comfortable in either setting, perhaps because their parents had shown them the way.

Having grown up without the benefit of a two-parent family, Merl was unusually devoted to his children and was present for them in every sense of the word. He was their cheerleader, their disciplinarian, and the person they looked to for answers. He treated the girls and boys much the same. None were spared his hand if they were punished, nor were they denied his affection. For the boys, baseball provided an obvious point of connection. The girls, it turned out, were pretty good with a bat too, playing softball and showing arms that would lead no one to say they "threw like a girl." Jill Eberly was an exceptional athlete and a collegiate-caliber runner; her father helped her train by riding a bicycle alongside her to pace her and almost never missed one of her meets. There is a photo in the Eberlys' home of Jill crossing the finish line after winning a race, her face and body forming a portrait of exhaustion. Merl's lessons about leaving it all on the field applied to daughters as well as sons.

Merl's bond with Rick was especially strong. He taught Rick how to hunt when he was barely five years old, but he always told his son to pursue the sport with a purpose beyond killing. He taught him to respect the land on which he hunted and to always find and remove his prey. Hunting also taught patience and focus, as well as the virtues of solitude only found in nature. Merl had dedicated his life to the proposition that his children would never struggle as he did and never head down the path to ruin that had nearly consumed him. He taught his kids the value of work. Rick and his sister Julie would both push the lawn mower, an old rotary blade model. Rick would shovel sidewalks and once unloaded a train car of old newspapers for 25¢ an hour.

Julie said her father was a "stickler for rules in all aspects of our lives." One day she left school fifteen minutes early to be with her mother and cousin for lunch, with her mother's permission and a note for an excused absence when she returned to school. Julie forgot, however, to sign out, and the school rule was that students could not leave early if they did not do so. Pat was fine with it, but Merl was not. He made her go back and take her punishment. She had to walk to school, a mile away, an hour early each morning until she had served her eight hours of detention for her lone high school offense. She did not resent her father for making her do it; she respected him for it.

He was unyielding. On Saturday mornings Merl would sound reveille from the bottom of the stairs to wake the kids for chores. The girls were not allowed to date until they were sixteen. Then they had an 11:00 P.M. curfew, and to Merl that did not mean 11:01. "He was strict," Joy said. "We knew our boundaries."

He was just as unyielding in his approach to baseball, not to show players how much he was in charge but rather to show them the value of discipline. "He utilized baseball as a catalyst to give back, to teach life lessons," Joy said. "It was his platform to teach kids about life. You will have disappointment. You have to work hard for what you have. Nothing is free in life. You've got to earn it. [Those are] the lessons he taught us as well."

There was no ambiguity in his ways. He had a temper, was very opinionated, and was not a person, Joy said, to hold back on anything. "He didn't make it easy for us at times," said Rick, a man who is economical with his words and rather introverted for one who became a coach himself. One day Merl took Rick down to Campbell's hardware store and bought Rick a mower on a monthly installment plan. Rick had a dozen yards to mow, and he paid his father back that first summer.

His father imbued Rick and the other children with a work ethic, respect for other people, and an understanding that the customer is always right. There were fun times too, as when Merl carried Rick on his shoulders when he was a child while covering a sporting event for the newspaper. The kids also loved piling into the station wagon to go see Merl play for the town team, and they expected their dad to hit a home run almost every game. When Rick was older and occasionally got into some kind of trouble, he remembered the advice his father had given him: "If you end up in jail, don't waste your call on me." Merl warned the youngest, Rodney, "If you come home with a tattoo or alcohol on your breath, don't bother."

Rick's professional career, like his father's, lasted just one year. He had shown great promise during his junior year at Texas Wesleyan: in one week alone he hit six home runs and six doubles and batted in twenty-one runs. Scouts were taking notice. Being drafted after his junior year could mean a sizable signing bonus and a path that might take him even further than his father in baseball. Then, with one violent swing of the bat, Rick felt his knee pop out. In a cast down to his ankle for six weeks, he missed the rest of the season. His hopes for a professional career weren't over, but they were deferred, and his expectations had been reduced. To restore his game, he returned to Clarinda to play for the A's that summer, when his fluid swing came back. But in his senior year he mainly served as his team's designated hitter.

Still, Rick had proved he was a professional-caliber hitter, and he was invited to a tryout with the San Diego Padres, where Ozzie Smith was now playing shortstop. The day before the major league draft, representatives from the Toronto Blue Jays called Rick and told him they would be selecting him in the later rounds. He was thrilled because, as a senior, particularly one recovering from a serious injury, he knew his opportunities were limited. But then the Blue Jays didn't draft him after all. He was crestfallen. Soon his college coach called, though, and said the Blue Jays would sign him as an undrafted free agent assigned to the team's Class A minor league affiliate in Medicine Hat, Alberta, Canada. Rick said he signed for "basically a plane trip and the opportunity." He had only been to Canada on fishing trips. As it turned out, he didn't like the town, the playing conditions, or the cold. The whole league was in mountainous areas. Many of his teammates were young Latinos, seventeen or eighteen years old, from the Dominican Republic, and he had trouble communicating with them and relating to them. "For the first time I was uncomfortable playing the game," he said.

He was still having troubles with his knee, and now his shoulder began to bother him as well. It was difficult to get the ball across the diamond from third to first. One night he dove for a ball and partially dislocated his shoulder. He faced the choice of so many minor leaguers who get hurt: do you tell your coach and risk losing your spot, or do you try to play through the pain? He remembered the story of his father getting beaned and bloodied in a minor league game in Nebraska, then refusing to leave the game for treatment. "I was pretty well brought up that injuries are part of athletics," Rick said. "You aren't going to let that beat you." He tried to keep playing. "If you weren't out there, someone else was going to be," he said. "I was playing hurt most of the time. I was never 100 percent."

He couldn't throw well the rest of the season, but he hit .276 and led the team in RBIs. For the Blue Jays, it wasn't good enough. Assessments by major league teams are bloodless, and the talent pools are deep. Why take a chance on a guy who has had serious injuries — even if he can really hit — when there are dozens like him to choose from? Rick's manager called him into his office and told him he was being given his release.

The game that had been so much a part of Rick Eberly's life had now brought him low. He didn't think it was fair, but he knew that nobody ever promised him that it would be. He had been so close. What would have happened if his knee hadn't given out? He might have had a chance to play with Ozzie again. As it was, he was consigned to the same fate as his father.

Rick took the Blue Jays' decision hard, and he was more bitter than his father had been when released by the White Sox. He went far away, to Louisiana to work in the oil fields. "I just think I needed to get away," Rick said, "and find myself again. It was a pretty rough crowd in the oil field, but there were some good people too." He spent three years working in Louisiana and "sowed some wild oats." He followed the A's during the summers, and after a time he realized that he was missing baseball, even with all the pain that it had caused him.

Baseball, Rick realized, meant more to him than simply the long-shot possibility of wearing a professional uniform. He called his mother and asked if she thought Merl would be upset if he quit his job and came home. Rick knew that Merl didn't tolerate quitting. Rick said he missed seeing his younger siblings grow up. Merl and Pat had bought a shoe store, and Pat told Rick he could come help her run it.

But Rick found the job hopelessly boring. Like his father, Rick's passion was baseball. He started to play for the A's again and also helped his father coach. They found comfort and pleasure in the game's natural rhythms. "It's something that stays with you when you do it that long and that hard," Rick said. "It's just a love for the game, the people you meet. It's a fraternity, probably like no other."

Fortunately for Rick, Merl's reputation as a coach was such that he often received job inquiries from colleges. When Tarkio College, forty miles to the south in Missouri, contacted him, Merl saw an opportunity, not for himself, but for his son, and arranged for Rick to get an interview. When the Eberly men arrived on campus, they saw the potential players, a lot of kids with beards and bandanas, a stark contrast to what Merl demanded of the A's. Merl asked whether they were ready to play ball or go to war. Dick Phillips, the school admissions director, talked to both Eberlys, but Merl did most of the communicating about what kind of program his son would run. Players would be clean-cut, play hard, and respect the game, he promised Phillips.

After Rick took the job, he found little in the condition of the field to inspire confidence that this aspiration could be met. The infield at Tarkio was pitiable: it had no grass. Rick wanted to upgrade it so badly that he went to the local bank and took out a personal loan to cover the cost. His father, who knew his son couldn't afford to take on that debt, was not pleased. But Pat challenged her husband, saying, "At whose knee did he learn that if you want something badly enough, you are willing to make some sacrifices?" Merl loaned his oldest son enough money to pay off the bank loan, then extended him credit at a much lower rate of interest.

The year before Rick took the job, Tarkio's record had been one win and twenty-eight losses. During his first year, they improved their record to 10-15. Then they won three straight conference championships. Rick Eberly had found his calling in coaching baseball.

Like Scotty Kurtz and Merl before him, Rick also continued to play for the A's. The league permitted non-amateurs to be on the roster, and Rick kept himself in good enough shape that he could still keep up with the college players, especially with a bat in his hand. He continued to play for his hometown well into his thirties.

One of his teammates, Livin, could easily see in Rick's approach to the game just how much Merl had passed on to his son. From the moment he arrived in Clarinda, Livin had sensed Merl's devotion to the game. The fact that it was such a family affair only added to the appeal of playing for the A's.

"Merl loved baseball," Livin said. "That was it. He loved kids. He loved watching guys learn the game. And he loved the town. He loved what it did for the town. Bringing in kids and letting idiots like me see what Clarinda and the Midwest had to offer. That's why it's so easy for me to send kids there. You come back enriched. You learn so much more than the game of baseball."

Merl didn't have a star system on the A's. He treated the worst player as well as he treated the best. He knew that players, parents, and coaches had trusted him when they sent their sons to play for him. "Merl always felt the responsibility that went along with that," Livin said.

Just as he had done with his own children, Merl made his players understand that they would become what they worked for, both on and off the field. In his first summer in Clarinda, Livin baled hay by day and pitched by night. "That eliminated the glamour part of the game real quick," Livin said. He did well enough to attract interest from professional scouts and came back to Clarinda for a second summer. Livin's job that summer was to help sell ads for the newspaper — that is, until he wrecked Merl's car. Merl was angry at Livin but said very little. Livin had a knot on his head from the accident so large that he could hardly put his hat on that night. But he was scheduled to pitch, and he knew he couldn't face Merl if he didn't take his turn in the rotation. "He said, 'How are you doing? Go get loose,'" Livin said. "I couldn't see the plate. But you rarely said no to Merl."

Facing great competition, Livin's talent blossomed that summer in Clarinda, and his mental toughness grew as much as his physical tools. He pitched 75 innings, striking out 58, with an ERA of 3.96. He did so well that he made it to the Astros draft list, played four years in the minors, and reached Double A before turning to a career in coaching.

Many years later, Livin had a player who was a prospect with much higher potential than he'd had himself. Andrew Cashner was a big, rangy kid whose fastball could reach the upper nineties. He was a raw talent, though, and while he was a good kid, he also had a bit of a wild side off the field. Livin could have sent Cashner anywhere. He chose to send him to Merl. "That was the easiest thing in the world," Livin said. "I thought it would be a great fit. I was always cautious who I sent. I want them to be good people. I feel like I always owed that to the Eberlys."

The lessons Livin learned from Merl transcended what happened on the diamond. During a trip to Hutchinson, Kansas, Livin and several of his teammates were at a Pizza Hut, wearing their uniforms, for a postgame dinner. They were of legal drinking age, and they had ordered several pitchers of beer. They would tease each other by saying, "There's Merl at the door," knowing that would inspire fear. They kept making the same joke, and one player doused himself with beer. It was a great running gag until the man with the broad shoulders and the look that could kill walked over and said softly: "How are you boys doing?"

Merl and Pat had come for pizza too. "I want to see you boys in the morning," he said before leaving the restaurant, never raising his voice. The next morning Livin and the other players walked into Merl's motel room and saw five bus tickets sitting on the bed. Merl looked them straight in the eye and said: "You have a decision to make right now."

The dramatic gesture had its intended effect. Merl had that kind of impact on his players. They never wanted to disappoint him. "I felt like I had just let down the pope," Livin said. "And how was I going to explain this to my parents?"

Merl knew that he hadn't lived a perfect life himself, and he knew that these were college-age men old enough to legally buy a drink. At the same time, he always emphasized that the players were representatives of the program and of the town wherever they traveled. Merl could tell that Livin and his teammates understood why he had those rules and how genuinely sorry they were. Their baseball careers, in many respects, hung in the balance.

"He called us all back after the game and said, 'I believe you guys deserve a second chance.'" He told them they had let him down and endangered the integrity of the program. "It really dawned on me how that guy meant it," Livin said. "For that second chance I am forever indebted. Whether he was bluffing or not, I don't know. To me, he was dead set on it."

Dave Baggott, another player of that era, could relate. He arrived in Clarinda from his college team at Long Beach State, a self-described "punk" from California "who looked at life from a different perspective." When he arrived, Baggott's campus cool outfit of camo pants, a pink oxford button-down, and a brown tweed sport coat was not exactly the image Merl wanted his players to project, and he let Baggott know. "When I first arrived in town, my read was, 'Does my college coach hate me?'" Baggott wrote later in the A's newsletter, *Dugout News*. "Don't get me wrong. For many of us ballplayers, Clarinda will probably be the smallest town we will ever visit in our lives. We are just as amazed by you and your lifestyle as you are with ours. To say it was a culture shock was an understatement."

As the summer went on, Baggott, like so many other players, came to like his surroundings. Rick Eberly taught him to fish at Cecil Sunderman's pond. Baggott's summer job was baling hay, until he found out he was allergic to it — the hay, not the work, though maybe a little bit of both. After a day of taking a decongestant to stop his sneezing, Baggott could barely play that night. "Merl asked me what was wrong. I explained the situation. He promptly had me put on a jacket (it was only 90 degrees that night) and run laps around the ballpark for the remainder of the game — about four innings. I don't know if I sweated it out, but I never let Merl know if I took even an aspirin for the rest of the summer."

Later in the season, he would need much more than aspirin. As the team arrived for the NBC tournament in Wichita, Baggott and the others were anticipating the opportunity to play in front of dozens of professional scouts. But Baggott felt miserable: he had contracted a severe virus that affected his brain. He had to spend the first six days of the tournament in isolation at the hotel, and he lost ten pounds. Finally, the medication that doctors gave him started to work, and he told Merl he was ready to play. Merl was dubious but put him in the game, knowing how much it meant to players to have this kind of showcase.

Baggott was weakened, and his thinking was hazy, and his uniform was suddenly baggy on his frame. In his first at-bat, he drew a walk, but was soon picked off first base. Later, he let a routine fly ball go over his head, resulting in an inside-the-park home run. Merl took him out of the game in the middle of an inning, a profound embarrassment. In the moment, Baggott was furious. But over time he came to see the situation in a much different light. "Here's a guy who knew how sick I was, who knew how weak I had become," Baggott said, "and yet he still gave me the chance in the most important tournament for a college player next to the College World Series. I know that I had no business suiting up, but Merl knew how important it was for me."

Overall, Baggott's time in Clarinda paid off. That summer he hit .291 with only 22 strikeouts in 141 at-bats, to go along with 23 stolen bases. Based on that season and his college play, Baggott signed a professional contract and played for two years before starting a career as a coach. After that, he became part of the group that owns the Ogden Raptors in Ogden, Utah, where he is now the one providing the small-town atmosphere for baseball fans.

Merl was as special to the people of Clarinda as he was to his players. The attention he'd brought to the town had enhanced its sense of identity, and he did it all on his own time for no compensation. When General Mills, the makers of Wheaties, sponsored a national contest to put a local hero on a box of cereal, Merl was the town's obvious nominee. "We collected the box tops and sent them in," said Venita Muller, who helped coordinate the campaign. "We set out empty Wheaties boxes and asked people to join in on this. I would collect them and send them in. I don't think we got close, but it was fun doing it. And the paper picked it up and put an article in that said everybody should eat their Wheaties. He is very worthy of having his face on the Wheaties box." A company representative even called Muller to ask her why entries for a person from a small town in Iowa were coming from people who said they lived so far from there. Muller explained about the A's and the college players coming from all over to play baseball in Clarinda.

Muller was not the only one who felt that Merl had put so much into the community that he deserved anything he could get back from it. His bonds with his neighbors were so close that they were like family to him. Merl had gone to high school with her husband, Lloyd. When Lloyd was going through a serious surgery while Venita sat alone in the hospital waiting room, in walked Merl to be with her until the procedure was completed. "I said, 'You didn't have to do that. Not even my family came.' And he said, 'We are family.'"

Merl was also the town's number-one sports booster, attending the games and matches of the boys and girls in Clarinda, offering them support, whatever the sport, whatever the season. He would send Venita and Lloyd's daughter Heidi articles about sports and encouraged her to pursue her passion for basketball and volleyball. She did just that, all the way to a college scholarship.

All the while, he maintained relationships with former players, both those who had become stars and those who played their final game in college. When the A's 1982 season ended, Ozzie Smith's big games that year were really just starting. He had found new fame as the All-Star shortstop of the St. Louis Cardinals, but he did not forget the couple who helped him get there. When the Cardinals made it to the World Series in 1982, Smith made sure that he secured tickets for Merl and Pat Eberly and invited them to stay in his home.

Merl and Pat drove to St. Louis, about six hours by car, arriving at Smith's home in the area known as West County outside of the city. After a while, Smith began unpacking boxes of card tables he'd bought to make it easier to serve food for all of his guests. As he was unpacking one of the boxes, a large staple jammed into a finger of his throwing hand. The All-Star shortstop was about to play in one of the most important games of his life, and his finger was bleeding profusely. The freak injury not only might be enormously embarrassing to him, but also could cost the Cardinals dearly.

Merl took a quick measure of the situation and asked Ozzie, "Do you have a lemon?" Ozzie wasn't quite sure what his old coach was thinking, but replied yes, he did. They cut off the end of the lemon to expose the fleshy part, and then Merl told Ozzie to stick his bleeding finger into the sour fruit. Ozzie did. There was a sharp sting from the citrus, but he kept his finger in there overnight. The next day there was very little swelling in the finger, no bleeding, and no soreness. Merl was a folk doctor along with being a baseball whisperer.

8

No Bright Lights

CHUCK KNOBLAUCH PACKED his bags in College Station, Texas. He had completed his freshman season at Texas A&M, where he'd validated his reputation as a player with major league potential, one who could hit for power and average along with being a great fielder. Well known in Texas, Knoblauch had been drafted out of high school, and his reputation was spreading. He carried himself with a confidence on the field that betrayed his youth. That first year at A&M, Knoblauch had played center field as he continued to recover from a broken leg. Now he was headed to Clarinda, Iowa, where he would get back to shortstop, his preferred position, and the one most scouts thought he could play in the majors.

Andy Benes was coming from his sophomore year at the University of Evansville in Indiana; the six-foot-six pitcher was traveling to his summer home with his new wife, a first for the A's. He was raw but talented, and finally starting to focus on baseball. One of his college teammates at the University of

Evansville, Rob Maurer, a first baseman, was making the drive west as well.

Scott Brosius was traveling from the west, from McMinn-ville, Oregon. He had played at an NAIA school, tiny Linfield College. Brosius was a blue-collar player who ran hard on every play and constantly worked on fundamentals, the kind of player Merl Eberly hoped for every summer. He also conveyed a sense of confidence and maturity that the others instantly noticed.

Cal Eldred's trip to Clarinda was comparatively short, just under five hours from the tiny Iowa town of Urbana, a place that celebrated things like "Sweet Corn Day." His family had a hog and cattle farm there. Eldred was a six-foot-four pitcher who also had been drafted out of high school but chose college at the University of Iowa, where he had completed his fresh-man year. His coach, Duane Banks, knew that his young pitcher would be well cared for and well coached by his friend Merl Eberly.

Then there was the hitter that everyone seemed to be talk-ing about, Nikco Riesgo from California, a player who already seemed fully developed physically and stood out even among a collection of young stars. Riesgo, who had been a high school All-American, played at San Diego State and was named a freshman All-American by *Baseball America*. He was the player Merl thought had the best shot at the big leagues.

Most of these players had not heard much about their team-mates. This was 1987, in the pre-Internet era, when cell phones were rare. Reputations were earned in real time. In many ways, that was an advantage to Merl: the players knew little more about him than what their coaches had told them. He respected the players sent to him, but no matter who they were, they had to earn their playing time with the A's and avoid running afoul of his rules, which were as clear in 1987 as they were the year the A's began. "I remember him bringing a credit card to a game and checking our faces to see if we had shaved before the game," Benes said. "I had really not had any coaches that were that meticulous about facial hair. I think he commanded that type of respect because he followed the same standards we were asked to. There was no double standard. He led by example. A few of the guys tried to boycott that rule, but eventually they realized it was follow the rule or hit the road. And our baseball careers were ahead of us."

Knoblauch, who stood only five-foot-eight, said Merl was physically intimidating to him. "He was a big man, with big old hands," Knoblauch said. "He was just a sweetheart of a man, but he was a tough baseball coach. I respected him instantly." Like Benes, Knoblauch knew Merl would neither brook dissent nor tolerate prima donnas. "He understood the nuances of baseball. He insisted you play the game hard. He wanted you to run every ball out, to hit behind the runner, to execute the hit-and-run. He didn't stand for any nonsense on the field. There was an aura about him."

Benes was initially advised to leave his wife at home, because of all the time the team had to spend on the road and other demands of the game. That lasted all of ten days before Jennifer Benes came to join him. They had an apartment instead of staying with a host family. It was certainly true that Benes had little time away from baseball, and it wasn't the easiest start for the newlyweds. He had a job in a furniture store during the day and was at Municipal Stadium or on the road for long stretches for the next three months.

"I developed as a person, and that was a very demanding summer," Benes said. "You worked all day and played ball at

night. I matured as a young adult. I learned responsibility working at the furniture store, and I learned how to be accountable
on the ball diamond. That is what Merl demanded. Being accountable for what you do is something that many do not want.
I had a job to do at the furniture store, and I took great pride in
that. I worked for a nice man, and that was his livelihood. I had
responsibilities, and I wanted to make my boss proud. You get
out of things what you put in. I took that mind-set into what I
do on and off the field. I didn't want to let down myself or anyone else."

How Benes arrived at Clarinda is a longer story. It begins
with his college coach, Jim Brownlee, who earlier in his career
coached at Illinois State. In 1974 he became the manager of
the Galesburg, Illinois, team of the Central Illinois Collegiate
League, a collection of college summer teams much like the A's.
Brownlee had heard about Merl and the A's after Ozzie Smith
played there. He later met Merl at the annual baseball coaches'
convention, and theirs became a decades-long friendship. At
first Brownlee hesitated to send players to Merl for a simple
reason: he didn't think his guys were good enough. At the same
time, he also knew how valuable a summer in Clarinda could be,
so he kept searching for players he could send to Merl. Brownlee's "philosophy" was that if you're sent to Clarinda, "you are
going to find out if you really want to play baseball. It was like
the minor leagues. Bus rides. Every day using a wood bat and
facing good pitching. Lots of guys would realize, 'This is not the
life for me.' Merl was going to make them work. I am old school,
he is old school."

Brownlee also liked the small-town quality of Clarinda. "You
couldn't get into too much trouble in Clarinda," he said. "And

having players live with people — I liked that. It was not only a baseball experience, it was a life experience."

For the six players arriving in Clarinda and the rest of the team that year, it was a time of testing. The Jayhawk League in 1987 was filled with future major league players, so every night they would be facing essentially a version of a college All-Star team. These six young men also dreamed of making it to the big leagues, and had that potential, but so did almost every player who came to Clarinda or played for one of the other teams in the league. An overwhelming number of them would find out that summer how shockingly small the odds were for stepping onto a major league field. "When you are playing every day like that, it's not like college with one or two games during the week and three games on the weekend," Knoblauch said. "We only had one or two days a week off. The more you play, the more reps you can get, the better you become. You were seeing different pitchers. It seemed like the summer leagues had a different style, harder throwers."

When Brownlee sent Benes to Clarinda, it was with some trepidation. At that point, "he wasn't a top prospect, he was just okay," Brownlee said. But Benes was a tremendous overall athlete. He had arrived at the University of Evansville as a quarterback recruit on the football team. As a freshman, he also played basketball and baseball, something almost unheard of at that level by the mid-1980s. He'd had an unremarkable freshman year, and during his sophomore year he'd had only an average fastball. Brownlee decided he should see what Benes's potential was in Clarinda.

That summer would be the first time in his athletic career that Benes had made baseball his sole focus. He started to throw harder as the summer wore on and to gain confidence. He threw more than he ever had before, almost seventy-seven innings over the summer. At the National Baseball Congress tournament that summer, his fastball hit ninety miles an hour for the first time, and professional scouts in the stands were impressed. One scout from the Phillies said they would be following him in the spring to gauge their interest in drafting him. Benes started to throw even harder.

Once Benes had talked with the scout, he called Brownlee and said he was giving up the other sports to concentrate on baseball. Brownlee knew the football coach would be steamed, but he told Benes he had to call him. Benes did, and the football coach was in fact furious.

The decision changed the course of Benes's life. Starting after the summer in Clarinda, Benes played fall baseball and maintained a consistent throwing program for the first time. By the next spring with the University of Evansville, he was routinely throwing ninety miles an hour. At a college tournament in Wilmington, North Carolina, Benes was set to face Georgia Southern, and the stands were packed with about thirty scouts, including several cross-checkers — advanced scouts sent to verify initial promising reports. After Benes warmed up, his pitching coach turned to Brownlee and said, "You aren't going to believe this. Benes is going to put on a show." His first pitch was ninety-four miles an hour. "He had never thrown that hard," Brownlee said. "He struck out twenty-one of twenty-seven with only eight breaking balls."

Benes, who had been a biology major, now knew he could make a living as a baseball player. Both he and his coach traced his rise to his summer in Clarinda. Life slowed down for him in the small town, and so did the game. He started to think of his life as a newly married man and the obligations that went with it. Without the distractions of college, he had time to think. At Merl's direction, he took everything about the game more seriously, from how he warmed up before a game to the workouts he did between starts to help restore his body and build his strength. Like so many former catchers who became great coaches, Merl had an easy connection with pitchers.

"Merl truly cared about his players, far more than just on the baseball field," Benes said. "In some ways he was training us for life, through the vehicle of baseball. Most of the guys were done playing ball within several years of their time in Clarinda, but Merl was always concerned for the guys regardless of whether or not baseball was a career path post-Clarinda. He kept in touch with many of the players long after they finished playing. Merl treated players with respect and was demanding, but did so in a gentle way. He didn't need to yell or scream to make his point."

Merl's passion for baseball endeared him to coaches who shared it, like Banks, who also admired the enduring quality of the A's program. "Getting a team going in a small town is difficult, but he did it right," Banks said. "He was very proud of the fact that he was able to help kids. Everything he did, it seemed like it was for everyone else and never for himself. That's what coaches do — put everybody in front of themselves. You would never know if he was having a bad day." Getting a team started, Banks said, was one thing. It was keeping it going that was the real miracle in Clarinda. "I don't know how in the world he did it. I think he had some mirrors."

Banks was highly confident when he sent Cal Eldred to Clarinda after his freshman year. Eldred was a small-town Iowan from a family of quite modest means, but he was also a kid who had a rocket arm and could play other positions on the field besides pitcher. Eldred was comfortable in Clarinda, not put off by it like the players coming from California or from big cities. He was relieved when he and Maurer were assigned Merl and Pat as host parents and they could make their new home in the basement on Lincoln Street. At that time, he felt that he often could relate to coaches even more than his teammates. The other players teased him about the challenges of staying with Merl, with all those rules. "I was like, got something to hide?" Eldred said. "The coach is going to find out what you are doing anyway living in a small town."

Merl also knew that Eldred really needed to work that summer to earn money. As the third of six children, Eldred said that the only way he was able to attend college was with a baseball scholarship. So Merl placed the farm kid at the local John Deere dealer, and the fit was natural. He was soon polishing combines, moving junk piles, cleaning up, and mowing. To Eldred, it was just like home.

Among these players, Eldred was hardly a standout. He found himself sitting on the bench for the first time in his baseball career. Sometimes he served as a bullpen catcher for Benes. His break came when another team arrived with only eight players and he was asked to play first base to fill out their team. He smashed a line drive that broke the cheek of his own teammate. Only then did he start to get innings on the mound.

For Eldred, though, baseball was only part of the journey. He also carefully watched Merl and Pat, how they interacted, how they rolled with adversity, how they laughed, and how they talked. He learned as much from living with his host parents as he did from playing ball at Municipal Stadium that summer.

Benes also ate many dinners at the Eberly home on Lincoln

Street. He saw how Merl and Pat always tried to have at least one family meal a day, often feeding not just their own family but a number of players as well. In their interactions, he saw the genuine affection the Eberlys had for each other. "It was warm and comfortable to be there, and Mrs. E was always so kind and loving to the boys on the team," Benes said. "Dinnertime seemed special to me because the family gathered and it was a time to spend together. Meals there were wonderful, and the family was so tight-knit, they made each and every one of us feel as though we were part of their family. That is quite a feat when there are twenty to twenty-five new guys there each year.

"Merl was certainly the patriarch and had a deep love for his wife and family. They meant the world to him, and his eyes lit up and he was genuinely joyful with Pat and the kids. There was great conversation at dinner, as this was before the technology boom with smart phones and Internet. Just a different era and a refreshing one that my family tries to emulate, especially with all the distractions of life and technology and the fast pace of life.

"That home on Lincoln Street was a place of solace and a place for guys to see what marriage and family was all about."

Eldred had a serious girlfriend at the time from back home. She was two years younger than him, and neither of them liked being away from each other. Merl knew of this relationship from Banks, and he talked with Eldred about it frequently. "Merl had little bits of wisdom," Eldred said. "He would tell me, 'You better let her know how much you are falling in love with the game.' Then Mrs. E would always try to smooth it over. But I knew he saw ability in me that my college coach and high school coach did." Even so, during that summer, he said, "I wasn't good enough to be one of the main guys on the staff."

Merl did see Eldred's potential, but he wanted the pitcher to know the price he would have to pay if he wanted to pursue professional baseball, including the possible effect on his family. He conveyed to the younger man just how hard the work ahead of him was, not to scare him but to prepare him. It was the kind of conversation that Merl always wished someone had had with him when he made his own journey through professional baseball. In those days, though, personal considerations were considered quite secondary. "He knew what being a small-town kid from Iowa was like," Eldred said. "We talked . . . he said, 'Look, there are long bus rides, you don't make much money.' We talked about family, about how you have to figure that out. You have to decide what is more important, getting married and having a family and being around them all the time or being a professional baseball player and all the time that requires. He wasn't trying to persuade me to go one way or the other. He had been down that road himself. He had watched his sons. He had watched guys like Ozzie Smith and Von Hayes."

Merl told Eldred that, for him, family came first. That meant that he loved them first, and so his other major decisions always flowed from how he could nurture and provide for his family. "So by his actions and by his words, that's what he would tell us," Eldred said. "He would come out and say that. He didn't tell me I had to do that, but it was pretty obvious that if I had to make a choice, he would want me to choose my family over something selfish. And if you were going to choose a career in baseball and do all the things you need to do, you better make sure [your wife] knows that because she is going to have to buy in."

Merl saw a lot of himself in Eldred. After the White Sox released him, he could have tried to latch onto another team. Instead, he chose to build his life and family in Clarinda with Pat.

Baseball continued to dominate his life, just not in the way he had originally envisioned. Their marriage had endured because they had a partnership both on and off the field. For Eldred and his girlfriend, who would later become his wife, the summer in Clarinda helped them begin to establish the kind of trust they would need to make a baseball marriage survive. "I learned a lot from Merl and Pat about what a baseball family was going to look like," Eldred said.

Merl was always quick to acknowledge Pat's powerful role in the program. "Don't give me any credit for Clarinda A's baseball," he told the *Omaha World-Herald*. "If anybody is important to the A's program, it's Pat." He was being interviewed as he sat behind his desk at the *Herald-Journal*, having coached in Fort Smith, Arkansas, the night before—a six-and-a-half-hour drive away.

Merl had a natural affinity for Eldred, but he didn't have the same kind of personal connection with another of his players that summer, the one who seemed like a sure thing. Knoblauch had a Texas swagger, at least among his teammates, even as he was quiet and shy with his host parent. When you saw Knoblauch's skills, Eldred said, it gave you a hint of what it might really take to make it to the big leagues. There was good, and then there was Knoblauch.

While still in college, Eldred would get a taste of Knoblauch's talent on the receiving end. The Iowa Hawkeyes were playing Texas A&M, and Knoblauch had become an All-American. Banks told his pitcher that he thought Knoblauch was going to bunt, and he advised him to keep the pitch up so that Knoblauch would be more likely to pop up. Eldred followed his coach's instruction and threw a high fastball to his former summer teammate. Knoblauch had no intention of bunting and instead hit a three-run homer. "I said to Cal, 'What do I know?'" Banks said sheepishly.

Brosius was in Clarinda for only a short time—just five games—because he was selected in the twentieth round of the draft that year by the Oakland A's, with whom he signed on June 9. Even with so brief an association, though, Brosius saw what was special about Clarinda and the team that Merl had built. As he rose in his own baseball career he stayed connected to the Eberlys. Later he would send his own players for summer baseball in the cornfields.

When the season started, Merl was most excited about Riesgo, who was returning for another season from San Diego State. At the time, Ozzie Smith, Buddy Black, Von Hayes, Darrell Miller, and Mark Williamson were the only Clarinda A's in major league baseball. "There will be others," Merl told the *World-Herald*. "We think our next major leaguer will be Nikco Riesgo." He had good reason for that confidence. That summer Riesgo batted .354 with 14 doubles, 15 home runs, and 54 RBIs.

Merl had two other players he could count on that year: his oldest son, Rick, who could still swing the bat, and his middle son, Ryan, a player with professional promise of his own who had begun his career with the A's as the team's batboy in the 1970s. Rick hit .294 in the nineteen games he played and drove in seventeen runs, almost one per game. Ryan was starting to do a self-assessment, comparing himself to Knoblauch, among others. He knew he had a lot of work to do.

The team went 43-23 in 1987 and finished in the first division of the Jayhawk League, advancing to the fifth round of the National Baseball Congress championship. Merl had no way of knowing that this team would produce major league players, and in the moment that wasn't really his concern. The longer he coached the A's the more he was convinced that baseball was so much more than a game. For a few months in the summer, he had these young men, and he hoped to provide them with something that would long outlast their playing days.

"I think success is in this instance being able to give young men the opportunity to experience all of the elements," Ozzie Smith said. "Having to work during the day, play baseball at night, there is a growing that goes on in a little town like this that I am not sure you get anywhere else. And it prepares you not only for where you live but for life. The values in a place like this are values that stay with you for the rest of your life."

By this time, Merl was well established in the baseball world, with connections from the college ranks to the pros. At the NBC tournament in Wichita, he was treated like an honored guest and held court with coaches, scouts, and players. Coaches from top colleges would send him strong players, knowing that they would be in a positive environment, guided by a real baseball pro and given the opportunity to develop even more.

At that time, the A's were part of the Jayhawk League, whose teams were drawn from cities in the nation's breadbasket. Among the coaches in the league, only Merl did not accept any pay. "If I got paid, it would put too much pressure on," he said in an interview with the *Omaha World-Herald*. "And this is my hometown. I think it's good for the community and this is a contribution toward that. When I used to call players they would say, 'Clarinda, Iowa? Where is Clarinda, Iowa? Where is that?' Now I think a lot of people know where Clarinda is."

At the same time, 1987 in some ways marked the peak of the team, at least in terms of producing major league baseball players. The game was changing, and Merl's old-school ways were not necessarily what players were looking for. This was the go-

go, "greed is good" 1980s, and players were finding this middle-of-the-country hamlet and its stern taskmaster less appealing. In addition, scouts were shifting their attention to Cape Cod, with its vacation-like appeal, not to mention the fact that all the Cape Cod League teams played on fields no more than an hour's drive away from each other. The A's traveled hours on the Kansas Turnpike, and the Blue Goose broke down so often that players said they were on a first-name basis with local mechanics.

Butch Ghutzman, at the time the coach at the University of Houston, and a friend of the Eberlys for more than three decades, acknowledged that Clarinda "couldn't draw like the Cape Cod League." More and more as the years went by, he said, college players "were wined and dined. They had other options." Yet Ghutzman continued to send players to Clarinda, including Knoblauch, along with his three sons, to test their love of the game. "In order to know if you love this game, you have got to play in that kind of situation to appreciate what you have," he said. "You have to love the sweat, learn to clean your clothes, take care of your shoes, practice, play baseball with no fans. They don't have the bright lights and all that."

The 1980s were also a time of economic difficulty in Iowa as the state made the transition to an economy less dependent on agriculture. For many rural areas the financial struggles were unrelenting, and that made contributions to the A's all the more difficult to come by. Businesses were either contracting or being taken over by larger corporations. The neighbor-to-neighbor transactions that Merl had used for years to solicit money had become more difficult to complete. Merl even tried to persuade people in Clarinda that the players were helping to stimulate the local economy with their spending. "They will bring with them and spend a lot more money than they earn here and this should and will be a welcome boost to our sluggish economy," he told them. "Surveys through the years reflect players purchasing items such as clothing, gas, food, newspaper subscriptions, shoes and equipment to mention a few and so do the fans, friends and relatives that follow them here throughout the summer."

He made it clear that while all the local donations were appreciated, it was the more sizable contributions from former players that allowed him to have a budget to be competitive; such enduring ties to Clarinda showed the mutuality of the relationship. "A lot of young men who have gone through the program are now sharing in the expense of keeping it going, showing that it meant something to them when they were here even though they no longer play and surely folks in our community [are] much better off because they did and still do care," Merl said.

Even though the A's had been around for nearly two decades as a college team, Merl kept reminding the people of Clarinda to watch out for the players on an emotional level as well. "Keep in mind that the first couple of weeks are tough for these youngsters who are a long way from home and without friends," he noted. A player new to Clarinda "sees only new faces and another big athletic challenge in his step toward his goals. In several cases the young man has not been home since Christmas break." He conceded that the players "may seem different to us and they probably are. They are from all walks of life and from different parts of the country. They have come to Clarinda to be part of one team and that in itself is a tough challenge."

The constant financial pressure was one of many challenges Merl faced. He could count on getting money from Hayes, Gans, Black, and, of course, Smith, who that year hit his career-best

.303 and kidded his old coach for labeling him "all field, no hit." But people in the town were strapped, barely able to sustain their own businesses. A simmering tension began to be felt. But Merl wasn't afraid to confront it. "This past summer was a tough one for A's workers and hopes of some people helping out are voiced," he wrote in his column "Sports Shorts by ME." "It takes a lot of time and work when just a few have to carry the load. We feel the program is good for the whole community and would like a few more people to step forward and lend a hand. Anyone wishing to help out in any way will be welcomed as part of the program. Contact Eberly."

Merl didn't mind being the underdog. And he knew he wasn't going to change his ways or lower his standards or coddle some superstar. He had his sense of right and wrong, and that was that. He was teaching more than baseball.

"He welcomed players into his home and treated us as if we were family," Benes said. "Just his actions made people feel welcome. He had a genuineness that you just felt when you were around him. Merl taught us how to play the game with respect. How to conduct ourselves on the field. How to deal with umpires and the opponent. He demanded that we respect the great game of baseball and maxed out our effort when it was our turn to play.

"Merl was a father figure for so many young men," Benes observed. "He cared enough about us to teach us. He did this by his words and more so by his actions. Words can be cheap if actions don't match. Merl was a man of integrity. He did what he said he'd do. He taught us how to play the game and develop as ballplayers and young men, but did so in a kind way. A way that showed us he cared. He spent a lot of time with us and got to know us and what made us tick. Then he could relate to us in a way we could understand. And he did it with dignity and class."

Six players on the A's 1987 roster would go on to play in the majors. Only one Cape Cod League team from that year could make the same boast. Knoblauch was drafted two years later in the first round by the Minnesota Twins and was the American League Rookie of the Year in 1991. He would be named an All-Star four times in his twelve-year career playing for the Twins, the New York Yankees, and the Kansas City Royals. Knoblauch's Clarinda credential helped him when he first went to a big league spring training and both Ozzie Smith and Von Hayes talked to him about Merl and the A's. Smith helped ease Knoblauch's transition to the majors by talking to him about how to play the infield.

In the 1992 All-Star Game, Knoblauch and Smith were on opposing teams, Knoblauch playing for the American League, Smith for the National League. Knoblauch took a picture of the scoreboard with his picture showing, and his parents were there to share the moment. When he scorched a ground ball up the middle, he was certain that he had recorded his first All-Star hit. "Then Ozzie lays out" to get the ground ball and "throws me out," Knoblauch said. "Typical."

The year after his summer in Clarinda, Benes was the Collegiate Pitcher of the Year and a member of the gold-medal-winning U.S. Olympic team. He was also the first pick in the major league draft and went on to record 155 wins, with 2,000 strikeouts, including 10 in his professional debut. He had left the University of Evansville after his junior year but would finally earn his college degree in 2011 from St. Louis University.

Cal Eldred was taken as the seventeenth pick in the first round of the 1989 draft, seven spots ahead of Knoblauch, the player he thought had it all. Eldred pitched in the majors for fourteen years, for the Milwaukee Brewers, Chicago White Sox, and St. Louis Cardinals. He returned to his native Iowa once he retired from baseball.

Brosius went on to star for the Yankees as well, earning the Most Valuable Player Award in the 1998 World Series.

Rob Maurer played a year of major league baseball before returning to Evansville. His roadblock to the majors — during an era when an organization controlled a player's rights for six years — was that he was playing behind an even better first baseman, Rafael Palmeiro.

Nikco Riesgo, the player who stood above the rest that summer in Clarinda, also made it to the major leagues, playing for the Montreal Expos. A career that seemed to have so much promise produced one hit in the big leagues, a line drive up the middle off Frank Viola.

The success of these players would become a source of affirmation for Merl, who was starting to feel a cross-pressure in his own life as never before. His town and his world were changing at the same time. A new owner of the *Clarinda Herald-Journal* was consolidating operations, which invariably meant that there would be less local news in the only local newspaper. As part of an effort to cut costs, management decided that the paper no longer needed two advertising salespeople. So they turned to the man who had walked Clarinda's streets for thirty years, wingtip shoes shined, clipboard in hand, the one who had leveraged friendships into sales, and told him, coldly, that he was being let go.

Merl was stunned. He wasn't sure how many more years he wanted to work, but he knew that for a number of reasons he was not ready to retire, particularly not involuntarily. He fumed with resentment. This was not the Clarinda he had known, but with out-of-town owners, he knew there was really no one to fight for his job. This was an impersonal corporate decision. His job had fallen victim to the sweeping trend toward consolidation in the media business, often at the cost of coverage of local communities. The local stores on the town square had always been a point of pride in the community; so were the ads they placed in the *Herald-Journal* — a binding force in the community for generations — and the donations they made to the team.

Merl was seeing that when the owner of a business was no longer a neighbor, loyalties were lost as well. He had a small ownership stake in the paper, so he did receive a modest payout, but hardly enough money to retire on. He and Pat bought a small motel in town and tried to make ends meet by running it. His team was being threatened, and so was his ability to take care of his family, as he had counseled Benes to do. Merl liked to be in control, and now he clearly was not.

9

Opportunity

JAMEY CARROLL WAS just the kind of player Merl loved to coach. Not because he was big or powerful, not because of a can't-miss arm, exceptional power, or amazing speed. Merl liked Jamey Carroll because he really had none of those tools but no one ever outworked him. As a young college player, Carroll was listed as only five-foot-eight and about 160 pounds, so he did not stand out anywhere among the top prospects who played at major college baseball programs or produced eye-popping numbers at showcase camps. You had to watch him closely to see the nuance and subtlety of his play, even the way he ran off and on the field, to appreciate him.

For as long as he had played or coached or preached about baseball, Merl had insisted that players needed to honor the game and its traditions. No player ever earned the right to do less than his best. "Ninety feet!" he would yell. "Don't be a pansy!" "Hobby Dobby!" There was simply a right way to do things. Some players would roll their eyes — behind Merl's back — but to Carroll, Merl's words resonated. Carroll quickly came to realize that Merl was there every summer by choice — putting in all those hours, taking all those swings of the fungo bat, throwing all those pitches at batting practice, riding all those miles on the highways and county roads. Merl taught him an enduring lesson: Nobody will ever do the work for you. You have to own your work ethic.

Carroll was from Newburgh, Indiana, just east of Evansville, along the Ohio River. He was the middle of three boys in his family. They were all athletes and played whatever sport the season demanded — baseball, football, or basketball, the last being akin to religion in the state. Carroll really liked all these sports but over time gravitated to baseball. He kept a poster of a local hero, Don Mattingly, the New York Yankees star, on his bedroom wall. His older brother started to specialize in football and eventually earned a college scholarship. Carroll thought he might be able to do the same in baseball, and getting a scholarship would ease the financial hardship on his parents.

He had started his baseball career at Castle High School on the junior varsity team, but was called up to varsity during his sophomore season when an older player was injured. He did reasonably well and was starting to gain more confidence as a player. Carroll was primed for his junior year — the most important in terms of college recruiting — and had hopes of drawing interest. And even some major programs did show some interest. But while he was playing pickup basketball with friends, just weeks before the season was to begin, he took a turn jumping on a trampoline to give himself enough lift to soar above the rim and jam the ball through. It was the only way a young man of his height could dunk. He missed the rim and fell to the ground, suffering a compound fracture of his right arm, his throwing arm, and it looked as though his playing days might end in high school. His doctor told him he would never play baseball again.

Carroll was accepted at Indiana University and planned to head north to Bloomington, probably to study business. It was simply what fate had dealt him. By the summer after his senior year, his arm had healed enough that he could play one last season of American Legion ball. When he played well enough in a couple of tournaments to catch the attention of the coach at John A. Logan Junior College in Carterville, Illinois, about an hour west of his home, Carroll decided to take a shot at it. Junior colleges are proving grounds for some players who are overlooked by Division 1 programs and professional scouts. Carroll's play at John A. Logan attracted the attention of Jim Brownlee, the head baseball coach at the University of Evansville, and the same man who had coached Andy Benes and Rob Maurer. Brownlee offered him a partial scholarship, and Carroll transferred to the university, which was about ten miles from his home.

In his first season with Evansville, Brownlee said, Carroll proved to be "the best shortstop I ever had." He knew that Carroll wanted to play professional baseball, but scouts had told him that they thought Carroll was simply too small to play. Brownlee knew there was at least one good way to see if the scouts were right. As he had done for Benes — who was now a starting pitcher for the San Diego Padres — and Maurer, Brownlee sent his shortstop to Clarinda for the summer.

When Carroll arrived in Clarinda, he had teammates from San Diego State and Big Ten schools. It was rather intimidating at first. Always trying to be honest, he asked himself, *What do those guys have that I don't have?* Though Carroll came from a region that had produced a couple of major league superstars like Mattingly and Scott Rolen — who starred for the St. Louis Cardinals and the Cincinnati Reds — no one would have said Carroll's name in the same breath with those two. But even though he didn't possess exceptional physical skills, what scouts call "plus tools," Carroll had something at least as important — a "plus" heart. He worked hard and could do almost anything on the field with better-than-average skill, and he did the one thing any player can do right on every play and yet most don't — he hustled, relentlessly.

"I didn't know any better, or anything about it, I just wanted to play," Carroll said. "I hopped into the car and drove to a town that was even smaller than the one I had come from." Maybe Clarinda just looked that way. His hometown of Newburgh was actually smaller by a couple thousand people.

Unlike players who arrived in Clarinda and wondered at first if they had made a grave mistake, Carroll took one look at the surroundings and thought it was almost perfect. "You knew you were out there in the middle of nowhere playing baseball, and you are playing every day, traveling on buses — it was my first experience traveling that much — with a bunch of guys, and it was just baseball.

"You find out how much you love the game of baseball when you are out there," Carroll said. "There's not a whole heckuva lot else to do." Which was precisely what so many players came to find was Clarinda's virtue. Their coaches knew about it after sending players there, and professional scouts who toured the Jayhawk and MINK Leagues appreciated it, and the number of players who arrived in Clarinda with potential and left as professional prospects validated it. What Clarinda offered young players was all a matter of opportunity — getting a chance to play every day, to develop their game, and to be renewed with a sense of the possible.

Players such as Carroll are easily overlooked if they have not been able to play in Clarinda, where the everyday commitment to development pays off. There are thousands of college baseball players, and only hundreds are selected in the major league baseball draft. Of that elite group, only a few will ever step onto a big league diamond. In that context, Carroll's odds of making it were decidedly slim.

Yet Clarinda, as it had done for others, afforded Jamey Carroll the chance to test his limits. During the day he was on a painting crew that Merl had assembled; by the end of his first summer in Clarinda, he felt like he had painted half the town. Merl rode players about their work as much as he did about their play. He told them over and over that effort was important, that they were representing the A's to the town. If he thought they didn't deliver a quality paint job, they did it again, until he was satisfied. Not every player bought into the system, but Jamey Carroll did.

Carroll would get up in the morning, work on the painting crew with four or five of his teammates, and put in about eight hours. Then they would go to their summer home, rest for an hour or so, and head to the ballpark. Not that Carroll, who was hosted by the family of a well-to-do doctor, Bill Richardson, really had to rough it at home. Dr. Richardson's home sat at the end of one of Clarinda's boulevards and was one of the town's landmarks, a mansion by any standard. It also had the amenity of a swimming pool, the value of which could not be overestimated during the steamy days of an Iowa summer. But Carroll spent most of his time working, as an amateur painter and as an aspiring professional baseball player.

Summer programs have to strike a delicate balance. College coaches love the idea of their players getting additional competition and exposure. But they also don't necessarily want summer coaches changing a pitcher's mechanics or a batter's swing. Merl honored that, but he also commanded the kind of respect among both coaches and players that they rarely complained if he weighed in to help correct a player's flaw.

What's more, he had routines that Carroll came to embrace as vital to his development, even as his teammates moaned. Merl made Carroll and his teammates run ten sprints after games, which often ended shortly before midnight and came after a full day's work. Carroll is convinced that doing those sprints — with a purpose — made him a better base stealer.

He and his teammates also had to learn how to hit with wooden bats. Colleges made the switch to metal bats to save money. Metal creates the illusion of more power, but at the same time it allows mishits that lead to base hits — offense brought to you by better technology. The switch to wooden bats in the summer leagues (the A's switched in 1993) created tremendous separation between the real hitters and those who only thought they were.

Merl was ready to help players make the transition, and Carroll was ready to learn. Merl would put a batting tee slightly in front of home plate, and Carroll would take hundreds of swings. He learned how to really achieve extension in his swing; once he was successful at that, he could hit with a wooden bat and, in turn, could hit even better with a metal one. Carroll would go on to use Merl's drill throughout his career whenever he found himself in a slump.

Merl also emphasized the importance of learning how to bunt, how to hit to advance a runner on base, and where to position yourself on a cutoff. It was all part of becoming a complete player — and perhaps the only way someone like Jamey Carroll was going to make it to the big leagues. All the work only served to stoke his desire. "It made me realize how much I love the game of baseball," Carroll said.

"One part that I realized, [that] I took from being there, is that I am not the strongest or the fastest guy in the world. But one thing I can try to do is try as hard as I can and respect the game, and what I did learn out there was that by playing hard and respecting the game, and not wanting to let your coach down, learning that if you did not have a good day, you could add something and bring it to the team. I left there with a whole different appreciation for the game."

Merl's presence added to that feeling. The old coach had an aura about him, a combination of fortitude, elegance, and athleticism, even as he reached his sixties and seventies. He was a player's coach, and for three months he was also like their father. He carried himself with a sense of calm, and he passed baseball wisdom down like heirlooms, hoping that his players would do the same. Carroll and many others credited Merl with helping them become a man. Players also saw how other baseball people — whether an opposing coach, a general manager, or even an umpire — regarded Merl when they traveled to other parks. Merl didn't mind the attention, but he also saw it as an opportunity for people to get to see what his hometown was all about. He wanted baseball people to think of Clarinda when they thought of him.

"He had an understanding that families were sending their kids out there, that their kids were his responsibility," Carroll said. "And the town made it special. When you have something where people are volunteering their time, you realize how selfless these people are, how true-hearted they are, probably why I still have a relationship with my host family and with Mrs. E. Getting older and looking back, it's an incredible selfless act that shouldn't go unnoticed. They are caring people, and they loved to help out."

But that year also brought great tension. In 1994, the team had finished under .500 for the first time since 1957. Just as they were to begin competition in the National Baseball Congress regional tournament, a half-dozen players came to Merl and told him they were willing to play in the regionals but would not make the trip to Wichita if the team qualified. They wanted to go home. Merl's response was swift and clear. "Go to the clubhouse and pack your bags, you're done now." Merl could not tolerate their selfishness. He filled the roster with players from the 1970s, including his son Rick, Noel Bogdanski, Paul Homrig, Jeff Nichols, and, almost unbelievably, Von Hayes, who was willing to help his old coach after his own professional career had ended. (The NBC rules permitted former pros.) If Merl couldn't always rely on all of the young men who came to Clarinda, he had a core group who would always answer his call.

Pat Eberly, always a surrogate mother to the players who passed through Clarinda, completed the notion of family. She was the ear they needed, the hug they needed, and sometimes the truth-teller they needed. She also tolerated their many superstitions. For Carroll, it was a ritual with baseball-shaped bubble gum. When the A's were in the NBC tournament in Wichita, he would buy three pieces of gum from Pat for 15¢. When Carroll boarded the team bus, Mrs. E was there, and the transaction ensured that the ritual endured. "Stuff like that I love about the game of baseball, and that one thing made me bond with Mrs. E," Carroll said.

The A's were a family enterprise in other important ways too. Playing alongside Carroll were Ryan Eberly, who had been released by the Yankees, Rod Eberly, the youngest of the Eberly children and the one with the most baseball potential, and B. J. Windhorst, the first Eberly grandchild to play on the team.

Windhorst and Rod Eberly were both gifted athletes, and in the summers they played with Carroll they were also better hitters than him. In fact, Carroll was maybe the fourth- or fifth-best player in the A's lineup. Still, he was among the most valuable to the team because, as a leadoff hitter, he always seemed to find a way to get on base. "He was the best leadoff hitter I ever played with," Windhorst said. "If he didn't get on base — which he often did — he almost always saw as many pitches as you could as a hitter. It seemed he always ran the count to a full count before walking, getting out, or getting a hit. My grandpa loved that about him! He made pitchers work, and he was a tough out! Jamey was the kind of player that exemplified what my grandpa wanted in a ballplayer wearing an A's uniform and representing Clarinda."

Windhorst was nearly six inches taller than Carroll and outweighed him by forty pounds. Any scout looking at them side by side would naturally be drawn to the bigger player. But Windhorst saw in Carroll something major league scouts would eventually see: Carroll played with ferocity. He never took a play off, never assumed an out or a hit. And in the dugout he was a great teammate.

"He was small, not all that fast, and relied on instinct and smarts to be a great player," Windhorst said. "By no means at all did anyone ever see him making it to the big leagues."

It was Rod Eberly's first season playing for the A's after attending their games for the first eighteen years of his life. Like his brother Ryan, he had served as a batboy and taken many bus rides with the team, an experience that helped make him even closer to his father. Rick and Ryan Eberly had both signed professional contracts and played a year of organized ball, but Rod probably had the highest potential to go to the majors. He could hit the high-caliber pitching he faced that summer, but he clearly was still learning the game. And one of the people he learned from was Carroll.

"He played second or short, and everything he did was at full speed," Rod said. "And he could do all the little things, the intangibles." Every starting position player on the team that year went on to sign a professional contract, but Rod admitted that he wasn't sure at the time that Carroll would be one of them. "He embodied everything my dad preached," Rod said. "Discipline, fundamentals, control your effort, because effort is the one thing you can control. You can control how you show up every day on the field. He was a 110 percent guy all of the time. He was very competitive. He hated to lose, a lot like my dad. He didn't just say you need to hustle, he did it."

For Rod Eberly, the season was important in another way: it was the first time he had been coached by his father. In Iowa at that time high school baseball was played during the summer to avoid the cold weather of spring, and because Merl was always with the A's, his youngest son rarely saw his father in the stands for his games — maybe twenty times in four years. Rod was not resentful. In fact, he had felt spoiled by coming from a baseball family. Going to a playoff or World Series game or talking to a professional baseball player was as familiar to him as a row of corn. Not only did he understand his father's obligations, he said, but "I wasn't playing because I needed Dad's approval. I loved the game."

Because Rod played most of his high school baseball in the summer, he was not scouted as a professional prospect, even though he had that kind of talent. So he decided, like a lot of top players, to attend junior college, at Highland Community College in Kansas, where his brother Rick was the head coach. He had an exceptional freshman year and thrived under his oldest brother's direction. Rick Eberly was extremely competitive and had lived the game the way Merl had taught him. That season clearly prepared Rod for playing that next summer for his father.

Still, he welcomed the chance to finally have the experience his brothers had had with his dad in the dugout. Rod was probably more talented than his brothers, but less intense; he actually enjoyed being coached, even if it happened under the sometimes harsh glare of his father. "I saw the fire he coached with," Rod said. "He was very intense. He wanted it done his way. Even looking at him as my dad, as a coach, his demeanor was so impressive to me. I remember being pretty in awe of my dad and wanted to please him, but he demanded it of all the guys."

Rod started that season in an unfamiliar place — on the bench, watching players like Carroll. Every regular position player but one on that team ended up playing professional baseball at some level. "That was a new experience for me," Rod said.

"I had always been 'the guy.' I had to learn how to speed my game up. I learned a lot from Jamey Carroll that summer. I realized you had to work every single day to get better. That really opened my eyes to how many good players there are out there."

Carroll played in Clarinda in the 1994 and 1995 seasons, and he could not have come at a better time for Merl. Over the years Merl had seen the game change. Players were more selfish and less likely to go along with what he saw as the game's essential folkways. There weren't many guys like Scotty Kurtz anymore who played the game out of a pure love for it.

When Carroll reflects back on his time in Clarinda, he sees that it had an even greater impact than he thought as a young man. He has come to appreciate that Merl was treating the college players almost as a professional coach would. You did your work as a player, but how you developed beyond that was your responsibility. Help was there, but you had to seek it out. The message to Carroll was clear: This is your career. How bad do you want it? "I felt like I got that type of discipline, and looking back now that was really incredible," Carroll said.

Merl knew that Carroll would not stand out to professional scouts for any single aspect of his game. He also knew that scouts could see desire and maximum effort, which, if combined with all-around skills, meant that a guy like Carroll could sometimes make it.

The year after Carroll left Clarinda, he returned to the University of Evansville for his senior year, still trying to show scouts that he was a professional-caliber player. Even though Brownlee tried to promote him, "scouts kept telling me he was too small to play." But a scout for the Montreal Expos, Bob Oldis, was finally convinced when he watched Carroll play a game against Creighton University in Omaha, Nebraska. First Carroll hit a ball to the hole at shortstop and made it down the line to first base in a blazing 4.2 seconds, beating the throw. Then Oldis's impression was sealed with his last at-bat. Carroll hit a weak tapper right back to the pitcher, one of the most routine plays imaginable. Oldis clocked Carroll running to first base. His time: 4.2 seconds. "Nothing stood out," Oldis said. "He just knew how to play the game."

The Montreal Expos drafted Jamey Carroll in the fourteenth round of the major league draft in 1996. He signed on June 20. For seven years, he played in the minors, often replicating his experience in Clarinda with the long bus rides, mediocre motels, and fast food. His coaches loved the way he played the game, and his teammates admired and respected him. Yet after that seventh season, playing for Triple A Ottawa, it seemed to him that it might be time to think about life after baseball.

After the season in Ottawa, he headed home to southern Indiana. Late in the major league season, when the Expos were playing the Chicago Cubs at Wrigley Field, one of the Expos' infielders, José Macías, broke his hand. The team needed a replacement quickly, and Carroll's phone rang. Among other factors, he was closer to Chicago than any of the other candidates. He said yes immediately and headed quickly north to Chicago. All the years, all the near-misses, sacrifices, and doubts, all of that was about to be washed away in one of baseball's most venerated stadiums.

On September 11, 2002, Jamey Carroll put on a major league uniform and walked onto Wrigley Field. His manager was the Hall of Fame legend Frank Robinson, a man of almost limitless ability as a player but definitely limited patience as a manager. Carroll delivered two sharp hits in his first game, and Robinson penciled him into the lineup for a second game. At age twenty-eight, in his second big league game, according to the *Washington Post*, Jamey Carroll was the oldest player in the lineup. He collected two more hits.

Carroll would never return to the minors. He went on to play with seven different teams through the 2013 season, with a career batting average above .270. To the surprise of no one in Clarinda, Carroll was twice nominated by his team for Major League Baseball's Heart and Hustle Award, which is voted on by active players and MLB alumni for the player "who demonstrates a passion for the game of baseball and embodies the values, spirit, and traditions of the game." When he was with the Dodgers, he won the Roy Campanella Award, which is given to the player who best exemplifies the spirit of the former Dodger catcher.

"When I walk away from this game, I want to be known as a good teammate and a guy who left it all out there," Carroll told his hometown newspaper, the *Evansville Courier & Press*. "When you get something like this that's voted on by your teammates you kind of have an understanding that what you do is appreciated."

His manager with the Dodgers was Don Mattingly, who grew up within twenty miles of Carroll in southern Indiana. Mattingly summed up Carroll's ability by telling the *Courier & Press*, "He's the guy who you don't truly appreciate until you see him play every day."

In the minor leagues, the story of Carroll has become the one that coaches use when players start to question themselves and wonder if the call will ever come. "Everybody uses him," Tim Leiper, Carroll's manager in the minors, told Adam Kilgore of the *Washington Post*. "He's the guy. He's the story."

In that same article, Adam Wogan, then the Expos' farm director, said that Carroll's overall skills made him indispensable. "He's so good defensively," Wogan said. "He can go anywhere. He's so sound fundamentally. I've never spoken to a guy that managed him that didn't say he absolutely had to have the guy on his team." The fact that the Expos were collapsing, Kilgore noted, probably enabled Carroll to get his shot. At his age, most organizations would have played a younger prospect instead of a player who seemed on his way to being a career minor leaguer. In the majors, Carroll played shortstop, third base, and second and hit .272.

"It seems like every manager he's ever had said, 'I need this guy on my team,'" Leiper told Kilgore. "So many things had to happen right for him to do it. No matter how many times he got kicked, he continued to work hard. So many guys would have quit." Carroll, Leiper said, didn't seem to know how to take a day off.

His best season as a professional came in 2006 when he hit .300 for the Colorado Rockies. In the 2012 season, Carroll signed a two-year deal with the Minnesota Twins that paid him $3.75 million in the second year. In the late summer of that year, the Kansas City Royals traded for Carroll. In the heat of a pennant race, the Royals' front office — people like Mike Arbuckle — went for the player from Clarinda who, as Richardson noted at Merl's funeral, always ran "as though the devil were on his heels." "I always felt like I was that twenty-fifth guy trying to make the team," Carroll told Kilgore. "And that's how I've always treated it."

Carroll's journey continued in the 2014 season, when he was invited to spring training with the Washington Nationals. Coaches put his locker next to that of Anthony Rendon, their promising infielder. Rendon said that he picked Carroll's brain every chance he got and told Kilgore that Carroll was "a great mentor to me." But even veteran players said that Carroll was a role model. Denard Span, the center fielder, said that Carroll had always been the kind of player who was ready an hour ahead of his teammates, every game. "He inspires me," Span told the *Post*. "Knowing how old he is and watching the way he plays the game, he never takes a play off, never takes anything for granted. I'm ten years younger than him. Whenever I'm sore or aching, I look at him and he kind of gets me going. Every team needs a guy like that."

One day before the Nationals broke camp, the team released Carroll, a decision that manager Matt Williams said was the most difficult one he had to make that spring. From 2002, when Carroll made his debut, to 2014, only three players who were twenty-eight or older at the time had continuously been on a major league roster: Derek Jeter, Ichiro Suzuki, and Jamey Carroll.

In Carroll's final game, on September 27, 2013, against the Chicago White Sox, he went 1-for-3. His last hit was the 1,000th of his career.

10

Stepping Off the Field

A S THE 1997 season approached, Merl Eberly was taking a measure of himself as well as his team. All the years of balancing the demands of his job, his family, and his beloved Clarinda A's were beginning to make his powerful shoulders sag. He finally acknowledged that he couldn't keep going as he had for the previous four decades. In addition to the physical and emotional toll, so many things were changing about the game that he was prompted to question his own commitment, something that had been unshakable.

He often used his column in the team newsletter, *Dugout News,* which was sent to A's alumni and supporters, to deliver an upbeat message about the team and its prospects or to tell a story about connecting with a former player, like Ozzie Smith. But this year the tone of his column was decidedly different, revealing an accumulated frustration. As usual, he confronted the situation with an unsparing bluntness.

"We, the Clarinda A's baseball program, are at a crossroads. Cutting back is not really an option anymore. We have done that for the last four or five years. Now, it's just a matter of getting financial assistance from our alumni if we are going to keep a competitive program — or perhaps even maintain a program, period.

"Baseball has been a part of the community for years, in fact since 1955, and there are not a whole lot of us from those early days still around. It's just the way it is, a fact of life that is no one's fault, but that is not the problem — increased costs and the dwindling of small community-based businesses is a large factor. Being in business myself I can certainly say that there are a lot more out there asking for contributions than there were in the past. It isn't even a matter of wanting more — we are at a level of trying to maintain."

He appealed for funds for a new scoreboard and new batting cages, really basic needs that would give the A's at least a hope of remaining on an equal footing with the other teams. He also acknowledged the economic transformation that was accelerating in Clarinda and throughout rural America. Small, locally owned businesses were having great difficulty competing against the big-box chain stores, and some people were starting to shop online, with their dialup modems that could take them anywhere in the world. The pace of life, even in Clarinda, was becoming more hectic. Merl was trying hard to make time stop, or at least slow it down, and there was a cost associated with that. "Any help will go entirely toward getting things back in shape in order to guarantee a longer future for other 'boys of summer,'" he said.

In Clarinda, there was always friction over whether to make the A's games an option that everyone could afford or to try to raise as much money as possible. Merl always chose the former. Season tickets for that year were $20 for an individual and $30 for a family, for thirty-one scheduled home games. But young families, who had been so essential to the team's success, were facing their own conflicts. It was now the norm to have both parents working, and children were indulging their own passions with time-consuming travel sports and other activities. You could also watch professional baseball on television almost any night of the week, so the A's had plenty of competition for people's time.

The A's decision to leave the Jayhawk League was having consequences too, even if, from Merl's perspective, it had been worth it. To comply with NCAA rules and be eligible for a subsidy from Major League Baseball, college summer teams could only have players on their roster who had at least one year of eligibility left. That left seniors and recent graduates with no place to go, even if they burned with the desire to keep playing, and Merl thought it was important to give those players that one final shot at a second chance of being discovered. To Merl, the Jayhawk League had become another "win at all costs" enterprise that put a premium on team revenues. The more flush teams had more than double the budget of others, and sometimes the A's disadvantage relative to an opponent was even greater. "That makes it tough too," Merl said.

It wasn't simply the finances. The players were changing too, and that weighed on Merl at least as much. Merl had played his first game at about the age of ten and would play competitively for more than thirty years. He loved everything about the game — the physicality, the mental dimension, and the lessons that carried beyond the field, like learning to deal with failure. He just wasn't seeing the same kind of pure passion for the game that he'd always had in the young men coming to play for him now. In another edition of the newsletter, his frustrations poured forth. "Could it really have been that long ago — that baseball was a game of fun," he wrote. "That it was played with excitement, with the true feeling of competition and love of the game being the biggest attraction — or is it the years gone by blur our memories of the 50s, 60s and 70s? I hope it is not the latter, because I know it was for ME [Merl always signed his column "ME" and referred to himself that way] and apparently for a lot of people who enjoyed competition — not always friendly on the playing field, but seldom carried off the field with you after a game.

"Why the change today? Maybe it's because many of the young people go at it year round, weight rooms, clinics, winter, summer, night and day.

"Maybe it's the money brought to professional baseball by big corporate owners selling entertainment, not just the game, but all of its surroundings supported by the commercial world of the media and the lines of promotion.

"Maybe it's the high school athlete and parents who think of the sport only as a way to a college scholarship — think a minute of division I college programs — big $$$ — or an eventual chance at the professional draft somewhere down the line.

"Don't misunderstand, money was exchanged for services if earned back in my era, pitching and winning could earn you up to $100, but losing was never rewarded with more than a thanks and expense money, enough for a tank of gas at .25 to .50 a gallon.

"That was thirty to forty years ago. Look at today when a young man can make millions before he ever swings a bat or throws a ball at the professional level if they are one of those chosen few. Where has the ethic of proving your worth before being paid gone? We all had dreams when we were young and rightly so, but I don't ever remember that I wanted to be Yogi Berra because of the money he made — it was because I loved the game.

"Many young people today are hoping and working year round for a scholarship and/or a professional chance to make a living in their chosen sport. They are not always doing it for the love and enjoyment of the game, but being pushed by society and the dream of big money robs them of young years when competition is supposed to be fun . . . When personal goals are the only reason for competition, then the team concept is gone and when the letter 'I' is inserted in the word team — the fun for all disappears.

"Coaches need to get back to teaching the game and let the athletes play as much as they can for themselves. It's hard to do for a society that demands winning in order to keep a job, but maybe then some of the right things that athletics should stand for can return to the front page of our sports sections and the game can be fun for all.

"Can this happen? I have my doubts, but it would be great if we could believe it would and the kids would all hustle in and out and pull for each other to do their best for their team's sake and not just for the MONEY that could be made down the road."

Those sentiments had been building for a long time. A year before, Merl had lamented that players were no longer willing to honor their commitments. "An ugly monster is raising his head — the behavior of the athlete, basically more off the field than his athletic ability. His commitment if you will. Coaches, I wonder what you are telling your athlete as you send him out to the summer program?

"Do you tell him that if he goes it is a commitment for the length of the season? Do you tell him that people open their homes for him and that he will have to go by their rules? Do you tell him that people work ten months to provide a summer program, raising funds, etc.? Do you tell him that nearly all the people volunteer their time and money? Do you tell him he is a guest in that community and his action on and off the field represent himself, his family and his school?

"Do you tell him that quitting is a step back for all involved? Do you tell him to contact you before making that kind of decision? Do you tell him that he is expected to hustle and abide by team rules? Do you tell him that he is to go all out, baseball wise, for only about four hours a day? Do you tell him that loyalty is important for success at any level of the game? Do you tell him he is going out to improve his skills — not to stay out till all hours? Do you tell him it only takes one player to ruin many years of efforts by others?"

The A's had had their share of issues — occasional drinking incidents, even more rare instances of drug use or players sneaking out to chase girls overnight — but considering the age of the players and that they were coming from a college environment, misbehavior was clearly the exception. One of the reasons Merl wanted the players to have jobs was so they would have as little idle time as possible. It just seemed to him that the players were now arriving in Clarinda with a sense of entitlement he hadn't seen in Ozzie Smith, Von Hayes, Buddy Black, or Darrell Miller.

"As far as I am personally concerned, I never met a young person I didn't like, but some summers have certainly been bigger tests on that sentiment than others and when the season is over, there are never any hard feelings, only a few disappointments.

"The way I see it — quite simply, either the athletes try to help summer baseball survive, both on and off the field, or in a few years it could be gone . . . If I believe in anything it is in the basic goodness of people and it is my hope that with help from all quarters the attitude and hustle will continue to bring many more memories of 'The Boys of Summer' in the years ahead."

No matter how low he was feeling, Merl wasn't ready to call it quits. He had a good group of players coming for the summer of 1997, and he would give them everything he had. Privately, though, he had come to a decision. This season would be his last as the field manager.

Rod was on the roster that year, ready for his junior year on a baseball scholarship at the University of Alabama–Birmingham — a Division 1 program consistently ranked among the nation's best at the time — and on the cusp of a professional baseball career of his own. The previous season at Highland Community College, Rod had 18 home runs and 73 RBIs in 56 games. He was drafted in the twelfth round by the St. Louis Cardinals, his favorite team. Both of his brothers had signed as free agents, but Rod actually had his name put up on a major league draft board. He said the Cardinals offered him $15,000, but Merl thought that was too low because the average bonus for a draft choice in that round was $30,000. The scout who had tendered the offer didn't budge, though, and Rod turned the offer down to head to Alabama.

That was also Ozzie Smith's final season with the Cardinals, and Rod, Merl, and Pat went to St. Louis in the late summer to catch a game before he headed back to school. The Cardinals' cross-checker scout, whose position far outranked that of the scout who had recommended that Rod be drafted, came up to Rod and Merl and said he was sorry they couldn't reach a deal; he told them he thought Rod would sign for $30,000. "What are you talking about?" Merl said, and they told the scout that Rod had never received the higher offer. "The guy was white as a ghost," Rod said. Apparently, the lower-level scout never conveyed the offer.

It was a moment that showed that for all of the Eberly family's connection to baseball people on every level, even they didn't get the full story about Rod until it was too late. They were too trusting in what the original scout said and didn't even think to bother Ozzie Smith by conferring with him about the offer. Years later, Rod downplayed the moment. "That was the one bad thing that happened to me," he said. "It was very hard for me to handle hearing that. I didn't process it until I was at UAB. And for the first six weeks or so, I couldn't hit. And I had always been able to hit."

Back at school, he struggled. He carried the burden of the reputation of one who had been drafted in the twelfth round and of the expectation that he would excel among college players. He was also thirteen hours from home and family, feeling isolated.

Then one of the coaches who had signed him to his scholarship, Steve Gillespie, who went on to be the head coach at Youngstown State, began to work with him one-on-one. Once again, an Eberly was redeemed by a coach. Gillespie made Rod work, tweaked his swing, and kept the pressure on him at just the right level. And Rod delivered. He hit .360 with 8 home runs and 60 RBIs. But the major league draft came and went again, and Rod Eberly never got a call.

He headed back to Clarinda to play for the A's that summer. For the first time in his life, his enthusiasm for the game was gone. He was disconsolate about the draft and about the Cardinals' handling of his situation the year before. His mood infected the team, which included a number of players who had dreamed of being drafted only to be disappointed. "We let it affect us," Rod said. "I was playing for what the game could give me instead of the other way around. It was my dad's last summer, and that was something I regret as a player and as Dad's son. Knowing it was his last year, why couldn't I have sucked it up? When you are young and dumb, sometimes you don't think of others."

The A's started league play that year a miserable 4-13. "Dad was tearing his hair out. He was pretty mad at us," Rod said. "He was questioning what we were doing." Merl put it bluntly to his players. "If you are not playing for love of the game to get better, why are you playing?" he said.

There was also a moment when Rod felt the full brunt of his father's wrath. Playing third base, with runners on second and third, he tried to backhand a ball when the proper play would have been to shift his feet and get his body in front of the ball, blocking it to prevent runs from scoring.

Merl was furious. This wasn't how he taught his sons to play. He got to the top steps of the dugout and yelled at his son. Rod looked at him and waved him off with his glove, a clear sign of disrespect. "Needless to say, he had some choice words for me when I got back to the dugout," Rod said. "He didn't care who I was. You were not going to be disrespectful to him."

Merl eventually got the team behind him. The A's went 14-3 in the second half of the season and qualified for the National Baseball Congress tournament, ensuring that Merl could have a well-deserved bow as a coach.

The tournament had its own special rhythm. Games were played around the clock, even if that meant starting at 2:00 A.M. That schedule was part of the charm, and part of the test. A photographer for the *Wichita Eagle* captured Merl in a pose after a fourteen-inning win against a team from Cape Girardeau, Missouri, a game that had started at 10:00 P.M. His arms are folded just below his chest. Despite the victory, he looks more frustrated than joyful. His lips are scrunched tight, and his cheeks are puffed. His eyebrows arch, pointing toward each other like the lines of a triangle. Something isn't quite right. The Eberly family would laugh at the photo for many years. They had seen some version of that look so many times, in so many contexts, over so many seasons of their lives. They knew that Merl was not pleased about something. He didn't have to say anything. You could tell by the look.

The story in the paper that day was a tribute to Merl and the A's. Word had started to spread during the season that this would be Merl's last as a manager, after more than forty years of wearing a uniform. Indeed, that year he was revered throughout the tournament, as a baseball oracle whose wisdom was sought. Everyone there knew that Merl had long brought something special to Wichita when he brought his A's, with their powder-blue uniforms and beat-up team bus. Even more revealing, however, of what Merl had built with his team and his devotion to his players, as the *Wichita Eagle*'s Kirk Seminoff noted, was that "the A's don't chop up their team in August to bring to Wichita a new 'best of' roster including players from other teams that didn't make the field. Instead Eberly believes in dancing with the one that brung ya." Merl didn't believe in gaming the system, and over time his approach had been validated: the A's were always competitive in Wichita.

In Wichita that year, other coaches, fans, scouts, and players all came to pay their respects to Merl. He had left a mark in Kansas as well as in Clarinda. But there was a sense of melancholy in the moment. In his sixties, Merl still looked good in his "uni" (every spring, if he saw that he was getting a paunch, he'd go on a diet of steak and grapefruit), but he had lost track of the number of fungoes he had hit, or the batting practice pitches he had thrown, or the hours he had spent standing in the coach's box at third base, or the lineup cards he had drawn up, or the pre- and postgame speeches he had delivered. He would miss all that.

Yet it was clear to him that this was the time. In addition to his frustrations about the game and the players, he knew that if the A's were to be sustained, he would have to take on the full-time role of general manager. The time that he had spent on the field would now have to be devoted to the perennial task of raising money and trying to keep the program alive. He had been doing both jobs for decades, but now he needed to focus on business even more than baseball if the A's were going to make it.

Merl was not the only one to see the threat to the A's. Ed Miller, who served on the A's board, challenged other directors to look at the steady decline in attendance at the games. "It's something we need to really think about, get out and visit with people about this problem," he said after the season had ended. "Right now, I don't have any answers, but it's something we have to come to grips with and what our next step will be if we can't come up with a solution. People are awfully busy in our fast-moving society."

Another longtime board member, Jim Thuman, put it even more starkly. "If we are doing all this work just for our own entertainment, then maybe it's time to move on. I ran the gate this year, and people just weren't there most of the time. Everyone seems to be doing other things than coming to A's games. It's kind of sad, but that's what appears to be happening."

Ryan Eberly suggested doing additional baseball clinics for

kids in the area to reestablish connections in the community. Others suggested that players be more active and visible in town. No one, however, really had the answer.

In his column, Merl implored the people of Clarinda to help come up with ideas "on what can be done to get people back to the ballpark." Perhaps, he thought, appealing to the comparatively pure and simple nature of what the A's were offering was a pitch he could sell. Major League Baseball was still dealing with repercussions from the 1994–1995 players' strike, and its relationship with fans was strained. If you loved baseball, Merl reasoned, why not see it at the amateur level where money was not the object? He said that the A's could still be a showcase for future major leaguers, as it had been. Just as important as financial support was more commitment from fans. Merl's players were starting to notice the empty seats at Municipal Stadium. It was "fans, or lack of them, [that] the players talked about," Merl wrote. "This summer was one of the lowest ever and the vets noticed it even more than the rookies.

"Baseball at this level is as good or better than the low minor leagues and is a real bargain for the fan," Merl wrote. "Families can come to every A's game for just a few dollars. It's a clean, wholesome atmosphere, no beer sales, great up close seats, good playing facility and the A's auxiliary does a great job with the concession stand. Baseball bingo was introduced this season."

He was offering an analog solution, however, in an emerging digital age. Some on the board of directors had a different idea for increasing revenue. They thought selling beer might be the answer. But there was no way Merl would go for that, and his view prevailed. In seasons to come, one of the A's biggest rivals, the Mustangs of St. Joseph, Missouri, just a little over an hour away, would routinely attract an average of two thousand fans to each of their games. One clear reason: a spacious beer garden. Many college summer teams are for-profit enterprises. The A's would never be one of them.

To Merl, success wasn't worth it if you had to do it that way. Just as John Tedore had given his life direction by showing him a positive path through sports, Merl saw baseball as a vessel for instilling larger values in his players. Even with the success his team had achieved and the small dose of attendant fame, he knew that the lore of the A's wasn't enough to attract a top prospect. At the same time, he had always known that the Clarinda A's weren't simply in the business of producing professional players: the team, with the people of Clarinda, was in the business of providing opportunity and molding young men.

"However corny it might sound, I think we're all supposed to do something while we are here on this Earth," Merl said in an interview with a local radio station. "I guess the good Lord took me out of the garbage can and said, 'Go play sports, but don't forget the message that it teaches you.' If you get the opportunity, pass it on . . . Try to be a little better person. Respect others, which we all need to do in this day and age. Don't do anything halfway. If you are going to do this or anything else you do in life, do it with passion. I think if we could do that in life, period, things would be a lot easier for all of us. It's not about can we make them a better baseball player. It's about can we make them a better person."

Indeed, while the A's produced an outsized share of great baseball players, many others who passed through Clarinda went on to excel in other fields — as doctors, lawyers, politicians, entertainers, and successes in business. There was Mike Sanchez, who went on to become a state legislator in New Mexico, and there was Cas Soma, the pitcher Merl sent home the year the A's won the NBC World Series, who became a successful surgeon in Hawaii. And of course, there was Danny Gans, who was packing in the fans for his Las Vegas shows.

As conflicted as Merl felt about the state of the game and the players, he knew in his heart that he couldn't stop being involved in baseball and probably wouldn't for as long as he lived. When word spread that he was stepping off the field, letters started to pour in from former players, as part of a project to provide a living memorial to Merl's work. When Merl read those letters, not merely from his players who went on to be professional stars but also from players whose lives were transformed, he realized that he had achieved his larger dream — to teach something beyond baseball.

One former player, Ben Snyder, acknowledged in his letter that his decision to come to Clarinda to play had not been easy. He had played the previous summer in Alaska. As a Californian, he was not exactly captivated by the notion of Iowa. But Von Hayes really encouraged him to travel to the cornfields, so he did.

My first memory of Clarinda is you walking down the stairs of your house and greeting me. You looked big, but gentle. I was scared and uncertain. I didn't know it right then but I was going to have one of the best summers of my life ... I learned to trust people and appreciate relationships. You set the example by caring more about me, the person, than me the pitcher. Second, you taught me to leverage my strengths and challenge the world. You always encouraged me to do so, especially after I tried and failed. And finally, I learned that I couldn't fool everyone like I thought I could. I needed to be true to myself and others. At times, I thought you had powers beyond any mortal: how else would you have known how late I was staying out at night. A lot of people know you as Merl Eberly, the baseball coach who puts together and manages great teams. But I know you as Merl Eberly, the man who changes lives.

Snyder's life was changed in another way by his summer in Iowa: he married a woman from Clarinda.

Terry Unruh's letter was handwritten in red ink and took up an entire page. "Some people are great because of what they accomplish and others are great because of what they acquired, but only a few are great because of what they have planted in the lives of others. Thank you both for being among those few," he wrote.

A major league scout, Bill Clark, who had come to Clarinda in the early 1970s, was ending his thirty years on the road and, like Merl, taking stock of his life. "In the wide-ranging view of this scout, there is no place in the world where baseball is more pure than in Clarinda, Iowa," Clark said.

Donny Carr, who had an outdoors business, recalled in his letter to Merl that his own father had taught him to

never allow anybody to have a great influence on my life without letting them know in writing how they impacted me . . . In your case, you were not only a friend over the years, but a great example of how to do life, and a consistent fiber in a world of inconsistency. I watched you share with others when I know you and your family were in need. I also watched you mold young people, like me, who were ungrateful and naive about the commitment you had to achieve the end result, which was good for me . . . one of my regrets is that I have waited this

long to let you know how much I look up to you. My respect
of your character and integrity, and the uncompromising conviction to what is right set you apart from anyone else I know.
This isn't intended as flattery Merl, it is said in sincerity because you have earned the right to know how much difference
you have made in the lives of many men.

To Jeff Nichols, Merl was "a player's coach," one who intui-
tively understood how a player could reach full potential.

As a player playing for a college coach who designed my style
of play, it was rather puzzling for me to play for Coach Eberly
for the first year. I didn't know what he wanted. Rather than
bunt, steal, hit and run he was telling me to focus and hit the
ball hard or look for that one pitch and drive it. In practice,
he mentioned the physical attributes that I had and asked me
why I wasn't using them, which made me really wonder. I fi
nally understood that he didn't want me to play his game, he
wanted me to play MY STYLE of baseball. That is a life lesson which has stayed with me, to take risks and explore my
abilities in whatever I do. It is safe to say I came to Clarinda
confident in my game and left Clarinda confident in myself. It
also let me know Merl Eberly doesn't just care about players,
he cares about people — that is not something you find in just
any coach. The only thing Coach Eberly wants from a player is
to respect himself, the community and the game. He is a great
coach but he is a better man.

Some of the letters also came from Merl's former teammates.
It was as though Merl was taking part in a living wake, but
hearing from those whose lives he had touched also affirmed

his decision to keep the program alive. "He gave me confidence in my ability to accomplish what I never thought possible," said former teammate Ernie Tomlinson. "He was so positive and so gracious. It demanded that you give your best plus another 50 percent because we knew he was giving that much and more. When 'Ebe' was behind the plate you could strike out anybody. You knew with one swing of the bat that Ebe could win the game for the home team."

Merl's impact on so many people came in large part from the way he honored the game's most sacred traditions. In addition, he asked his players to approach the sport with the same buoyant enthusiasm they'd had in their Little League days. Quoting from a baseball essay, Merl taught them that to play baseball you have to "carry that little boy with you in your back pocket."

Who could possibly carry on the tradition that Merl had built? The people of Clarinda knew that he couldn't go on forever. But the team and the town were stronger than one large man. As Merl readily acknowledged, Pat was his anchor. She was a master at logistics and details, and her relentlessly optimistic manner was infectious. The team structure was dated, and no doubt a bit sexist. Men were on the board of directors, and women were on the auxiliary. Pat in many ways had a foot in both camps, but in the 1990s the A's were a male-dominated enterprise, even though women played indispensable roles.

While the continued presence of the combination of Merl and Pat ensured that the team could go on, that still left a void on the field. Merl's sons were not yet candidates to take over the team, for a number of reasons. So Merl turned to his old friend Noel Bogdanski — a former teammate who had come to Clarinda from Chicago — to carry on the tradition. "Bo" Bogdanski was a big, strong man, much like Merl, who inspired respect.

"Taking over the A's is going to be a big step for me," Bogdanski said at the time. "I have some really big shoes to fill. I have been with the A's off and on since 1973 and have seen some very high moments and also some very low ones. Merl has taught every one of his ballplayers something while they have been here, dealing with life or baseball, and I hope I can do the same — even if it only stays with them a couple of days. As coach I plan on running the same tight ship that has been the trademark of the A's program."

Merl may not have been in the dugout anymore, but he was hardly away from the team. Instead, he transitioned into the role of a very active general manager. His presence was felt at every game as he stationed himself on a folding chair near the A's clubhouse along the left-field line. He had a clear view of the field, and he continued his practice of second-guessing umpires, coaches, and players. He didn't miss a pitch.

He tried to explain his feelings in his column, but only from a baseball perspective; his other feelings were too private. "Changing from playing to just managing was tough, but trying to help youngsters to be better players and better people became my goal — a great feeling when you see the paths many of them have taken and you feel you have succeeded more than you have failed. Winning was and is important, but even more important is to teach the players that the lessons they learn on the field can carry over into their lives and make them good people.

"It was me that made me step down. I had come to the age where it was really hard to physically teach and coach, and I didn't want the kids to have to suffer because of that . . . I just don't have the energy to do both the field managing and business end of the program. You bet I will miss it but 'nothing is forever' as the saying goes. You can't be with young people every day for three months each summer for as long as I have without some feel of loss when it's over.

"I am looking forward to devoting my time to assuring that the program will survive through the years . . . Being the GM will allow me to still be close to the kids and that's important to me. Why? Because I can truthfully say that I have never met a young person I couldn't like."

Rod Eberly went to spring training with the Phillies in 1999, played the entire spring season, and then was assigned to the New York–Penn League affiliate in Batavia, New York. As happened with his brother Rick, Rod's body was starting to break down. His knees hurt, and so did his shoulder. He played fairly well until the last month. He ended up hitting .220 and struck out three times in one game for the first time ever as a baseball player. "It was a humbling experience," Rod said. Still, the Phillies weren't ready to give up on him, and he was invited back for a second spring training.

The atmosphere the next spring was intense. Knowing that this was probably his last chance, Rod kept slavish track of his statistics. He was hitting nearly .400 with two home runs and 17 RBIs. "I wasn't the least concerned that I would be released," he said. Then, with ten days left in spring training, Rod was met by a trainer when he arrived at the spring training complex. "He said, 'The GM needs to see you,'" Rod said.

What would play out was a familiar scene for the Eberly men. "The guy sat me down and told me, at this point, it was a numbers game and they were going to have to release me, basically because of my age — twenty-three at the time.

"He said, 'You are a really good ballplayer,' and the only thing I said back was, 'Thank you for the opportunity, but if I were that good of a player, you wouldn't be letting me go,'" Rod said.

"I was pretty devastated about that. I had worked to the point that I knew what to do. I was 220 pounds and really strong. I really felt good about everything. I was just floored by that."

Merl called Mike Arbuckle, who was working for the Phillies at the time and had a long friendship with Merl. Arbuckle told Merl that the organization was concerned that Rod would not be able to hit. Merl wasn't buying it. "Mike, that's all he's ever done his whole life is hit," Merl said. But there was no reversing the decision.

Merl and Pat were in Florida at the time, visiting an old friend of the A's program, George Bradley, who was working for the White Sox. Merl arranged a meeting between Rod and Bradley, who told the young man that if he stayed in shape he could come to the White Sox spring training the next year.

Like he had done so many summers, Rod went back to Clarinda and played another summer with the A's. He did well enough to attract the interest of an Independent League team in Louisiana. The pay was better than the pittance he had earned in the minors, so he went. But after playing about eight games, he hurt his back and finally decided to give up his dream. He played one more summer for the A's.

Every Eberly man had traveled essentially the same arc in his baseball career. They were forged in Clarinda, first the father, then the sons under his direction. They grew to love the game. They flourished, to the point that they were probably better than only a small fraction of those who put on a uniform and advanced to the major leagues. They signed professional contracts and had their shot. They never made it beyond a low level of minor league baseball, but could always say they had played professional baseball. Then each of the sons came to see the game as their father did — as a way to teach values beyond sport and to stay connected with their family and their town.

From the time Merl took over as the A's manager in 1961 through the 1997 season, the team's record was 1,501–591, a winning percentage of .717. During its years as a college program, it was 1,219–507, a winning percentage of .706. As a player, Merl Eberly ranks only behind Von Hayes, who hit .511 in 1979. Merl's best was .475 in 1969, when he was thirty-five years old.

11

Keeping

PAT EBERLY APPROACHED the front door of Evelyn Herzberg's modest ranch-style house on Glenn Miller Avenue with trepidation and a hunch. Evelyn's husband had died only a month before, and she was still dragged low by grief. As it happened, Pat's daughter Jill was married to Evelyn's nephew Scott. Pat knew that Evelyn, who had no children of her own, might benefit from some company. She told Evelyn that a couple of Clarinda A's players would be arriving for the summer in just two weeks and wondered if Evelyn would consider taking them in for a short period while she searched for a family that would keep them for the rest of the summer.

Finding families to host players was, in many ways, as important to the A's success as finding players. Families had to be willing to take in total strangers, young men who would have to blend in with their children, abide by their rules, and behave off the baseball field. This was one of many ways in which Pat was as indispensable to the program as Merl. She had lived her entire life in Clarinda, and she knew which families she could count on to offer the right environment. It was never about which family could provide a player with the nicest home or the most amenities. Pat knew that the players arriving in town were complicated — they were excellent athletes with all the urges of young men, yet at the same time they were away from home and not fully adults, feeling insecure and, for some, even quite homesick. That required a special kind of family that could almost instantly trust and nurture someone they might never see again after the season ended. Some families would serve as hosts for decades, and others for a half-dozen seasons; for a smaller number, one summer was enough. In the early days of the A's as a collegiate team, some families resisted hosting black players, even those that had taken in foreign exchange students who were of color. Over the years, those issues went away. Like almost every town, Clarinda had its intolerant residents, but they were in the distinct minority.

The families of Clarinda referred to hosting players over the summer as "keeping" them. The term conveys the broader context of their responsibility and how they viewed it. They were not providing mere lodging. They were keeping the young men in the broadest sense — treating them as they would their own daughters and sons. Keeping meant providing emotional support and modeling behavior. For many families, it also meant financial sacrifice, at times when they could least afford it. Once Pat had the host parent program established, keeping the summer players was as integral to the A's viability as a program as Merl's connections with coaches. By participating, the people of Clarinda were also keeping themselves and their town connected. Most in Clarinda did not see this as remarkable. "To us, this is a normal thing," Evelyn said.

The program had certainly grown from the summer when Pat and Merl had to keep a third of the team living in their basement. Somehow, Pat managed to feed them all, as well as attend the A's games to run the concession stand. They had known that summer that this arrangement couldn't last, and that was when Pat started to form the host parent program.

She reached out to people like Larry and Shira Bridie, who owned Weil's, the local clothing store, and later Jill and Mike Devoe, who had their own two young children but felt a powerful pull to help both the players and their town. Pat enlisted Jeff Clark, who went off to college and came back to his town to put down roots, to give back, and to pass on the notion of keeping to his children. Like Jill Devoe, Jeff Clark was first exposed to the A's as a child. He would go to the games and run down foul balls and home runs. Each time he returned a baseball to the concession stand, Pat would give him a dime. As an adult, he stayed involved, helping rebuild the press box, putting a new roof on the dugouts, serving on the board of directors, helping out at games, and, foremost, keeping players.

Pat had a hunch that Evelyn would be wonderful at keeping, in ways that would benefit the players and the widow herself. But Evelyn had to give Pat's request some thought. What did she know about taking care of young men? She liked to cook and do craftwork, and she liked the Glenn Miller Festival and loved interacting with the Japanese tourists who were drawn to it. She also liked Pat and Merl, whom she had known for decades. She knew that if Pat was asking, there must be a real need, so she agreed to do it — she took the leap. "I had room," Evelyn said. "I was alone, and she was a friend. That's probably mostly why, trying to do her a favor. But the favor was for me because I always said it was a year of sorrow but also a year of joy because of all these kids through the years."

Two young men she had never met were soon to become like the sons she never had. She was responsible for them — caring for them, watching out for them, cheering for them, and telling them what to do and what not to do. She had to quickly establish a set of house rules and expectations, all without the benefit of experience. It was the start of being a "mother" for the next twenty summers.

Evelyn cooked for the players she was keeping and always made extra food for their teammates who stopped by. She tried to make it to their games so they would have at least one fan rooting for them. Although she had to adapt to this new responsibility, she was better at it than she first thought she might be. She learned the players' rhythms and learned to just listen. Evelyn also developed a sense of humor that others had never seen in her. She would play jokes on her summer guests. One time she sewed the pants legs of one player's jeans together, so that when he tried to hop into them, he fell to the floor. She short-sheeted their beds and put cellophane wrap on the toilet seat, which made nighttime trips to the bathroom hazardous. She played Scrabble, gin rummy, and other games with them. Deep and enduring bonds formed.

Somehow Evelyn's quaint approach worked, maybe even because it was quaint. These big, strong young men came to see her as, if not their mother, at least a favorite aunt. They knew her story too — that she had not had children and that they filled a void for her. They sent her presents and cards on Mother's Day and at Christmas years after they had lived with her in Clarinda and played for the A's.

One of the players Evelyn hosted was Chuck Knoblauch. Outgoing on the baseball diamond, he was reserved around her in her home. With her limited frame of reference on baseball, she really had no idea she was keeping a young man who had been pegged as a can't-miss major leaguer. "When I think of Evelyn, I can't wipe the smile off my face," Knoblauch said. "She was a prankster. She pulled all sorts of jokes on us. And she had us pick corn and green beans and make homemade ice cream."

The summer after he played in Clarinda, Knoblauch was named the best player in the Cape Cod League and also an All-American at Texas A&M. Within a few years, he was the starting second baseman for the Minnesota Twins. He became engaged and invited Evelyn to the wedding. She still keeps the invitation from him among her treasured cards, letters, and scrapbooks. Knoblauch also provided her with tickets when the Twins played in the World Series — a payoff she never expected when she answered Pat's call.

Evelyn also hosted Michael Strawberry, whose brother Darryl was one of the best players of his generation, and Patrick Dobson, the son of the actor Kevin Dobson, who starred in the television hit *Kojak*. Evelyn didn't know that much about Darryl Strawberry, but *Kojak* was one of her favorite shows. When Kevin Dobson and his wife came to see their son play, they stayed at her house for over a week. She did the cooking, and he bought the groceries. "He did the cleaning up," Evelyn said. "It was great. I was a guest in my own home."

Then there was Mike Humphrey, who played at Indiana University. He borrowed $384.24 from her to pay for his U-Haul. He paid her back only $100 with a money order. In his notes to her, he called her "Evvy Baby." "You have been like a mother to

me and I will always have a special place in my heart for you."
Another player, Justin Fitzgerald, signed a score sheet for her
with: "last game of Scrabble."

Evelyn was well aware that some of her players were sneak-
ing out at night or breaking Merl's rules of behavior, but there
were no serious incidents, and her players were often contrite.
One note said:

> Evelyn, I'm sorry about last night. I am sorry I let you down
> and it will not happen again. I think the world of you and your
> hospitality. You've made me feel at home and I thank you for
> all you have done for me and Pete. You will be appreciated and
> respected by me and Pete. Thank you. Chris and Pete.

Another, exhausted either from too much baseball or too much
of something else, simply wrote, "I am not going to church.
Please let me sleep. I am sorry but extremely tired."

Players came to rely on Evelyn as they would a parent. She
loaned one of them pots, pans, and kitchen utensils for his return to college. When another player broke his jaw in a game,
she drove him to Omaha to see a doctor. When her "boys" weren't
getting enough playing time, she would complain to Merl, just
like a mother. When they played well, she would make a sign
and put it on the front door to congratulate them, sometimes
even attaching balloons.

Not every experience was good. When one player broke her
rules, she had to get Merl involved. The player's father was a
high-powered lawyer and tried to steamroll Merl to preserve his
son's status. He was no match for the coach, though, and the
player was sent packing. Another player had a visiting girlfriend

and stayed out well past the 1:00 A.M. curfew Evelyn had set. She was going to send him home as well, but Merl asked her if she would give the player a second chance and she did. "It wasn't all peaches and cream," Evelyn said.

For Evelyn, though, the good far outweighed the bad. Clarinda families with children also saw the benefits of keeping a ballplayer for the summer, including the chance it gave their children to have an instant big brother and role model. And most of the time that was precisely how things worked out. Living in such a small town, people in Clarinda had relatively little exposure to people from other parts of the country, so keeping provided a form of mutual socialization — an opportunity to trade backgrounds, histories, and habits.

Beth and Brian Rarick had been keeping players since the late 1990s. The experience helped draw their own son, Sam, out of his shyness, and for that, Beth Rarick could thank a pitcher from the Los Angeles area, Jake Hovis, who embraced the role of mentor. Hovis thought that was the least he could do. He did not feel close to his own family at the time; in fact, he told Beth, he had "never really had a family-type situation like he had with us." A self-described "hot wire," Hovis was coming from a place with a much faster pace, and he found himself feeling grateful that the Raricks and Clarinda slowed him down. "In California, you don't have a second to breathe," he said. "And the first time I was in Iowa, I could look up and see every star in the universe. That was just earthly. At that point in my life, I was very fortunate to have the Raricks. I don't know if it was God or the Clarinda family, but I needed someone to take care of me. Anytime I struggled, they were there."

He delivered for them in the modest way they had hoped. He

did his best to bring out the introverted Sam, and the effort paid off. By the next summer in Clarinda, Sam was a "chatterbox," Hovis said. "I felt like I had a little brother and sister."

The Raricks gave Hovis quality time. They would wait to have dinner with him after the night's game so that he would have a familial experience. "I love my family to death, but they gave me another side," Hovis said of the Raricks. "I was not even their kid, and they were treating me like I am their son. They are asking me questions like they do care. They were genuine. That's what I miss. Just the genuine people."

Hovis carried that experience with him. After Clarinda, he was more sincere with people. If he asked someone a question, now he really wanted to hear the answer. He said the people of Clarinda had an "open-arms lifestyle" that he tried to adopt as well. "If someone is struggling, just open up your arms and smile." He is trying to practice Clarinda values living in California.

"I still appreciate everything that happened," he said. "Without those summers, I can't say I would be here . . . I don't want to know. If everyone went to play in Clarinda, this whole world would be a better place. You want to take that lifestyle and bring it back to everyone else. Everybody who has played there has a little bit of Clarinda in them."

Hovis was a pitcher with good command and solid potential, but wasn't drafted following his senior year at Concordia University. So he texted the Raricks: "When can I come visit you guys?" The Raricks did just what Jake Hovis had come to expect. "We found out he hadn't been placed," Beth said, "and we invited him to stay." After a second summer in Clarinda, Hovis landed a spot in the Freedom Professional League in Arizona. It wasn't the majors or affiliated baseball, but he was still getting paid to play.

While the families worked to put the players at ease, sometimes it worked the other way around. When a player from Arlington, Virginia, jokingly asked the Raricks, "Now, which part of town should I not go into?" they knew it would be a low-maintenance summer with him. Clarinda might have had a rough side of town when Merl was growing up, but that notion was somewhat laughable given the small size of the town. "I told him you can pretty much go where you want," Beth said. If there is a "good" side of town, the Raricks were on it, with a home alongside the seventh hole of the Clarinda Country Club. Players frustrated by baseball could take out some aggression banging golf balls if they needed to.

Sometimes Beth and her husband had to be sports psychologists. Players who were not succeeding on the field brought their problems home with them, and for some the pressure made them want to leave. She told them they had choices: "You can stick it out. Maybe you should look at it as if I'm getting some workouts, some team experience, a new experience." If they considered quitting, she would tell them, "We would hate to see you leave."

The host parents also could count on Merl weighing in. "If the team was down or the boys were having too much fun, then Merl would step in and you'd have the annual Merl Speech," said Brian Rarick, a podiatrist. "He always warned them about the age of the girls, and the curfews." There were times when Brian had to deliver the lecture to his players. "We usually have to give a little bit of 'Hey, guys, it's Clarinda, Iowa, not the city.' It's a small town, and we have our reputation."

The Bridies were important to the program on almost every level. They were among the first host parents and one of Merl's more reliable donors in town. "Most people knew when Merl was walking in, he wanted a check," Larry Bridie said. They also spoke up for Merl and the A's with other business owners and prospective host families. The players, Shira said, "really become part of your family. We looked forward each year, wondering who we would get. We opened our homes and our hearts. This is a nice way to live."

The time they spent in Clarinda was also a life internship for the players, akin to being on a cultural exchange program. Most of them had never been on a farm or driven a tractor — or even a truck for that matter. "The small-town atmosphere is different," Brenda Samuelson said. "There's no filter. They see it as it is, and most of them embrace it and just can't really believe it. Even the little things. We have an old beat-up pickup truck. Everyone has learned to drive a manual transmission."

Lloyd Muller, Venita's husband, would ask Pat every summer if any of the players would like to work on his farm, making hay bales, weeding soybeans, and digging post holes. (The family joked that the players were earning a PhD — a Post Hole Digging degree.) Merl approved of sending players to the Mullers: the work made them farm-strong. Venita would drive into town to pick them up if they needed a ride, then take them to the game if they worked through the afternoon.

"At first, it was kind of a trickle," she said. "They were city boys and coming out on the farm. They just didn't know. Then they discovered that the main meal at the farm is served at noon, so I did a lot of cooking." When that word spread, they had no trouble attracting workers. When the players arrived at the baseball field each night, they would taunt their teammates:

"What did you have for lunch today?"

"A sandwich."

"Well, we had steak and potatoes and corn and watermelon."

After lunch, the players would watch soap operas like *All My Children* or go into the yard to play Wiffle ball.

It was the players working for the Mullers who convinced Merl to break his tradition of having only boys serve as batboys for the A's. They could tell that Venita and Lloyd's daughter Andrea was a gifted athlete. According to Venita, "One noon when the boys were there, they said to Andrea, 'You can be our batboy.' I said, 'No, Merl only uses boys.'" That night when she went to the game, though, she saw her daughter carrying balls and bats on the field.

Venita also kept a player from New Orleans, but farm life was too much of a shock for him. He didn't like the smells, and he didn't like the work in the hot sun. He tried gardening for Venita, but was frightened several times by snakes. He preferred watching soap operas. "At my house, the kids all had jobs," she said. "We didn't sit around and watch TV, and I walked into the living room and turned off the TV, and I said, 'Larry, if you don't get outside and get ambitious and get things done, you're not going to amount to a hill of beans.'" He stayed just two weeks. But Venita was wrong about him, at least in one sense. The next year she opened a letter from him that included a newspaper article reporting that he had been drafted by the pros. "We got a good chuckle over that," she said.

Annette Nelson's family had five hundred acres and raised cattle, hogs, beans, and corn. Any player lucky enough to live with her for the summer got his fill of good country cooking. Annette was so adept at chicken fried steak that she made it for the team's annual Hall of Fame Banquet in the winter, which drew hundreds of people. Not surprisingly, Annette's home was known to players as "the food house." Over the years she kept more than forty players and always seemed to find room if Pat was in a bind. She kept boys because of her friendship with Pat and her fealty to the town. "I feel like I enjoy the summers having the boys. It makes me feel younger," said seventy-five-year-old Annette. "I tell them, 'When you come here, it's like staying with Grandma.' I just fully enjoy the atmosphere, being around the boys, going to the ballpark and helping where I can. I can't imagine a summer of not having that."

The keeping done by the people of Clarinda also had a powerful effect on the college coaches who sent players there. It created an environment where the players knew that people cared about them, and in turn they cared about the community. "Players felt an important part of that and came back with a sense of responsibility," said Augie Garrido, the University of Texas coach. "It was the entire environment. It isn't any one thing. It is a combination of all things."

That spirit was embodied by Evelyn Herzberg and by host parents like Jeff Clark, a lifelong Clarinda resident. He and his family hosted dozens of players over the years, and each summer he gave the players the same speech. "I have three rules. The first is that you will respect my wife and children. The second is, what is mine is yours. The third is, no spittoons in the house."

Clark admired Merl, both for the way he conducted his life and for the obvious closeness of his family. When Clark took on a task for the A's, he did so wanting Merl's validation for a job well done. He also wanted his own children to see how enriching it could be to give to others. After the A's games, Clark liked to sit next to Merl by the clubhouse and drink in his wisdom about baseball and life. "He was always coaching," Clark said. "Not only a coach on the field but off the field."

Like Clark, Jill Devoe inherited the tradition of keeping players. She recalled her father saying, when she was twelve, that they were going to remodel the basement because that summer they were going to host an A's player—the memory of whom she could summon with great clarity decades later. "Jeff Franks ... he got drafted that season. Catcher," she said. It was the start of having many brothers for the summer. She had been part of the A's for so long that she seemed to know no other way. "Foremost, it's the opportunity to develop relationships with people outside of Clarinda," she said. "It's the ability to expose the kids to different lifestyles. Even as an adult, I understand what it can bring to our lives as well as helping out others.

"As a child, it was fun. Big brothers play catch with you and do things with you. Just brought a whole different element to the summer. They had talks with me about guys and how to behave like a lady and what I should want out of life. My parents would have died if they would have known." Appropriately enough, players whom she had kept later called her for advice on relationships and life as though they were calling their own mother.

When Jill and Mike Devoe married, they knew that one day they too would host players—or at least Jill knew they would. Her parents continued to keep players until she was in college, and Jill and Mike decided to keep the tradition going in 1999, when their son, Jared, had just turned three. Mike, who worked at the local prison and had a stereotyped view of twenty-year-old males, was skeptical at first about having college-age men living in his house. "I had to twist his arm hard behind his back to get him to do it," Jill said. "He was like ... 'Why would we want to do that?'" But Mike was a baseball fan, though he'd never had a chance to play as a child because he was needed to work on the family farm. Eventually he agreed, and he and Jill became another generation of keepers.

The Devoes lived about ten miles outside of Clarinda, in New Market, a town of only about five hundred people that, among other things, took pride in its grand July Fourth fireworks display, which could easily be seen from the stands at Municipal Stadium. By comparison, Clarinda was a "big city." The players who stayed with the Devoes were almost certainly coming to the smallest town they would ever live in, but the way the Devoes approached their responsibility made these players quickly feel at home. They either had their own bedroom or shared space with another player in the basement. (The Devoes usually kept two players a season.) Jill and Mike were both classic Midwesterners — friendly, outgoing, giving, and very matter-of-fact. From years of experience, they knew how to draw a player out. Jill was also a prolific cook and highly organized, so their players always knew exactly where their next meal was coming from. Players could also count on seeing them at Municipal Stadium on game nights, and on the occasional road trip as well, particularly to Wichita.

The Devoes continued to keep players even when demands on their time were increasing. Their son Jared grew to the size of an NFL lineman and earned a scholarship to play football at South Dakota State. He was recruited heavily and had to be available for visits and tryout camps on the weekends. Their daughter Allie was an athlete as well and played travel softball during the summer. Jill and Mike found themselves shuttling from one event to the next. The "slow" pace of life in Clarinda was accelerating for some families. Still, the Devoes and others trying to keep up with their own families continued to serve as keepers, mainly because none of them could say no to Pat Eberly. "She keeps on you until you say yes," Jill said.

The Devoes continued to help in other ways as well. Mike

served on the A's board of directors, and Jill served on the women's auxiliary. Mike said that the A's survived over the years in large part because of the "circles" that Merl created among the people in town, his baseball family, and his own family, fueled by their strong desire to keep the program going.

Jay Moses served the A's in more ways than most. He hosted players, served on the board of directors, and ran J's Pizza & Steakhouse, the most popular eating establishment in town, located across the street from the Page County Courthouse. Players who stayed with him during the summer could eat at the restaurant for free. He had worked at the place since he was twelve years old and bought it on contract when he was only twenty-one. For more than thirty years it had been the most popular gathering spot in town. Jay had built a grand home across the street from Clarinda High School, and word would spread among players that his house was the best among host parents, complete with its own gym.

Jay had seen Clarinda from many sides. He had been a rather indifferent student at Clarinda High School but was the embodiment of the town motto: "Where the work ethic still works." He became both one of the town's most successful businessmen and one of the A's most important boosters. But he did more than write checks. He also did the hard work of maintaining the field, painting, and fixing fences, as well as carry out the time-consuming duties related to board meetings.

"I was born and raised here," he said, laughing. "I couldn't get away anywhere else." He didn't want to. "It's the way people treat you here. People are friendly and you get a lot of compliments. They let you know."

If a single family embodied the essence of Clarinda, it would probably be the Lisles. They founded a company, the Lisle Corporation ("the innovator in specialty tools since 1903"), on the eastern edge of town. Lisle's first product was a horse-powered water-well-drilling machine. The product line evolved and endured, even as the company dealt with competitors that paid their workers less and did not have comparable safety standards. Starting a job at Lisle could mean having a job for your whole working life. Scotty Kurtz had worked there more than forty years, ever since Merl brokered the connection. Mike Kurtz had worked there more than three decades. Richard Graham, Merl's childhood friend, worked there too. Lisle Corporation provided good jobs at good wages and somehow managed to win the battle against economic globalization.

John Lisle, who ran the company for several decades, exemplified the community pride that separated Clarinda from so many other places. An amateur historian, he had traced Clarinda's roots back 150 years or more. His personal archive of historical documents and artifacts showed how the town had changed — the businesses that had come and gone, like Grimes Rollerdome, the Frosty Shoppe, and Jed's Café — and how it had stayed the same, as evidenced by institutions like the county courthouse and his own family business. He had been witness to Clarinda's facility for "keeping," particularly with respect to Merl. "I don't think Merl could have prospered in a different environment," Lisle said, seated in his large, well-kept office at the factory. "These small towns are pretty nurturing. You grow up in one of these towns, specifically Clarinda, people know who you are. 'You play baseball.' It's always been a good atmosphere that way."

Bob Lutz, the sports columnist for the *Wichita Eagle*, was always impressed by the number of people from Clarinda who made the drive to attend the NBC tournament, many of them wearing the team's powder-blue colors. They decorated their cars, held posters in the stands, and cheered their "boys." "They must have different water up there," Lutz said. "Everybody I knew who was associated with Clarinda was one of the nicest people you can be."

12

Renewal

WHEN VON HAYES retired from baseball in 1993, it wasn't really by choice. He had been hit by a pitch by Tom Browning of the Cincinnati Reds on June 14, 1991, that broke his arm, and he would always feel like the injury never had a chance to heal. He returned to the lineup in September, and the Phillies traded him at the end of the season to the California Angels. Though he was on the downward plane of his career, he felt he had a few more good years left. He just needed another chance. But few baseball careers end well; almost all players are cut from a team or their contract is not renewed, and Hayes was no exception. As he put it at the time, "I don't feel like I left baseball, I feel like baseball had left me."

From early in his career, when the Philadelphia Phillies traded five players to get Hayes from the Cleveland Indians in 1982, Hayes had been burdened by outsized expectations. Fans didn't evaluate the trade in a sophisticated way. They simply thought that anyone good enough to be traded for five guys must be a superstar. His nickname—not one he treasured—

was "5-for-1." He was joining a team with one of the best major leaguers of all time, third baseman Mike Schmidt, and Hayes was supposed to help Philadelphia win another World Series.

It's never easy to succeed in Philadelphia or be popular with its fans, who, after all, are the kind who threw snowballs at Santa Claus during a Philadelphia Eagles game. When J. D. Drew refused to sign a deal with the Phillies after they drafted him in 1997, then later returned to Veterans Stadium to play as a St. Louis Cardinal, the fans tried to pelt him with D batteries. They were as unforgiving as any in baseball, and the City of Brotherly Love never really fell for Hayes. Sometimes it was Hayes who did little to draw the fan love. He had an occasionally brooding manner and would slam his helmet after striking out. But even when Hayes did the near-impossible — hitting three home runs in one game, and in another game becoming the first player in major league history to hit two home runs in the first inning — fans seemed to want more from him.

In his first three years with the Phillies, Hayes was a reliable major league starter, but not the superstar he had been projected to be. When the 1986 season started, Hayes felt confident that he could finally make that leap. He was told that season that he would be moving from outfield to first base — the position he played at Clarinda — and he felt good about that. But only days before he left for spring training in Clearwater, he learned that his father, the man who had taught him the game as a kid, was suffering from an incurable form of cancer. "Before I had left California for spring training I told Dad that I was heading for an MVP season," Hayes told Peter Pascarelli, the baseball writer for the *Philadelphia Inquirer.* "I guess I was trying to give him some incentive to keep going . . . but the illness took him." Hayes went back to be with his family and missed out on some of the critical time just before the regular season started. He would begin the year with eleven hits in his first eighty at-bats.

Nevertheless, he worked his way out of the slump. As Pascarelli wrote, Hayes retooled his swing, returning to the more simplified approach he had used in college at St. Mary's and during the summers in Clarinda. Hayes would go on to have his best year as a professional, even if it was not the joyful time he had hoped to share with his father. He had career highs in hits, home runs, doubles, RBIs, and runs scored. He batted third in the Phillies lineup. "If there is any justice, he will finish high in the National League's MVP voting," Pascarelli wrote. St. Louis manager Whitey Herzog said that Hayes had gone from "being a good player to being one helluva player."

Hayes would finish the season hitting .305, with 98 runs batted in, 19 home runs, and 46 doubles. He finished eighth in the balloting for the National League's Most Valuable Player, an honor won by his teammate Mike Schmidt.

At the time Hayes was a bachelor, and he felt an emotional void after his father's death, even with his success on the field. After the season ended and he no longer had baseball to fill the time, he knew where he could turn. He called Merl Eberly in Clarinda.

Reconnecting with Merl brought him back to the summer of 1978, when he took his first trip on an airplane, traveling from California to Iowa. During his first year in college, Hayes had grown four inches, and he was making the transition from shortstop to first base. He needed a summer program where he could learn the position. Some of his older teammates at St. Mary's recommended that he go to Clarinda, where they had played and had great experiences. His college coach, Miles

McAfee, also thought it was a good idea. Hayes was lacking in confidence when he arrived in Clarinda, though, and when he saw the A's starting first baseman, Tony Camara, he felt even worse. Some of the players were there from USC, San Diego State, Nebraska, and other power programs. Hayes lasted two weeks before deciding that it could end up being a long summer on the bench. He asked Merl for his release. "We'll let you go home because we don't really need you this year, but we would like for you to think of us in the future," Merl said, almost as a courtesy.

Instead of giving up, Hayes was motivated by his first brief experience in Clarinda. Determined to show that he could play with the A's, he worked hard during the fall and winter to prepare for his college season. The work paid off. After playing well enough at St. Mary's to be drafted by the Indians, he turned them down and opted instead to return to Clarinda, where he quickly evolved from a good to a great college player and his confidence continued to rise. Hayes would once again turn down the Indians when they offered him a better contract in order to help Merl and the A's at the National Baseball Congress World Series in Wichita. He hit well above .500 in the tournament.

At that point in his career, rather than see his stock go down, Hayes had a lot of baseball options, and Merl had helped him through it. Merl had never pressed Hayes to stay with the team when he could have signed a professional contract. He just laid out the young man's options and helped him gain clarity, and Hayes would leave Clarinda that second time with even more respect for his coach. "For me," Hayes said, "it was just his presence, his fairness, the way he treated everybody, whether it was his son Rick, who played on the team, or anyone else."

Hayes finally signed with the Indians in 1979, and during his first season in Cleveland the team traveled to Minnesota to play the Twins. Hayes, who was starting in right field, looked into the stands and there were Merl and Pat Eberly to cheer him on. "It was a pretty special experience," Hayes said. "My parents were back in California, so to have your surrogate parents there was pretty special."

As he progressed in major league baseball, Hayes found himself almost every year back in Clarinda to help his old coach, the team, and the town with raising money. They needed him, and he was there to help. He would also call Merl on occasion just to talk baseball and life.

After the 1986 season, even with his career-best statistics to that point, Hayes really needed Merl and Clarinda as he dealt with his father's death. He traveled to Iowa, where he decided to buy a piece of hunting ground a few miles outside of town, with Merl as a minor partner. He hadn't grown up as a hunter and really didn't know much about it. Once again, Merl became Hayes's coach and teacher. Merl talked to him about respect for both the land and the animals they were stalking, and Hayes learned the peace that comes from spending time in nature, with no distractions, just walking and talking with a friend.

Hayes would spend a few weeks each year in Iowa, where he was recognized everywhere and treated as a pleasant combination of celebrity and friend. Clarinda was about as far away from the Philadelphia fan experience as he could get. At first, he bought the land so that Merl could enjoy it with his sons and grandsons it was only later, when his own life had its troubles, that he came to see it as a place to call home.

Hayes credited Merl and the people of Clarinda with launching his professional career and felt an obligation and sense of loyalty to them long after his playing days were over. When the Phillies traded him in 1993, effectively ending his career, it was even more important that he could rely on other points of connection in his life to help get him through it, and Clarinda was one of those places. "It evolved to more than a player giving back, into more of a union between a player and a city," Hayes said. "I feel like [Clarinda] is a second home. I never gave up on baseball, but there comes a time when baseball basically lets you go. I never gave up loving the game."

After his father's death, Hayes eventually came to see his relationship with Merl as akin to that of a father and son. The annual banquet, the hunting trips, and the dinners with Pat and Merl and members of the Eberly clan all gave him a sense of belonging. The Eberly girls were his close friends too, and Hayes became something of a fourth brother to them. Hayes gained strength from the values that Merl and Pat exhibited, reflecting a kind of religious faith that, as he put it, they "didn't wear on their sleeves" but rather lived by example. The Eberlys were always there for him, even if he just needed someone to talk to. Today Hayes tells his friends that Iowa is his home and he is an Iowa resident. They don't always believe him.

After his professional career ended, Hayes knocked around in a variety of businesses. One of them was trying to sell boats in Florida. "One thing I learned about the boating industry, it's tough to sell boats," he told MLB.com.

He was married and soon would have two children. He introduced his wife Stephanie, an actress, and his kids to the Eberlys, and for a while they too were part of the extended family. Their family photo appeared in the A's newsletter, *Dugout News*. In addition to trying to sell boats, Hayes explored ways to leverage his status as a former big leaguer in other occupations. He met with mixed success, however, and never really found anything that compared to his passion for baseball.

After more than a decade of marriage, Hayes and his wife went through an acrimonious divorce that left him financially and emotionally scarred. He drifted. Whatever his difficulty, though, Hayes always knew where he could go when he needed support. He would travel to Clarinda and enter the back door — like all the other members of the family — at 225 East Lincoln Street and know that he'd find people there he could lean on. Merl would have a strong handshake for him, Pat would deliver a warm hug, and Hayes would feel his troubles start to melt away, at least temporarily.

"They were there to listen but not be judgmental," Hayes said. "They were very careful about being critical with their advice. They would always take my side. Their concerns were more for what was happening to me as a person in those tough times. I can't tell you what that meant to me." Sometimes Merl and Pat would risk disagreeing with Hayes and tell him to consider both sides of the story. That was part of their love for him too.

In few places did Hayes feel as welcome as he did in the Eberly home, where he could eat at the kitchen table or plop down in a recliner and watch a game, sipping iced tea, talking with Merl or Pat or one of the Eberly children, who always seemed to be streaming through their childhood home. "He had a special relationship with my dad and mom, and they always kept him grounded and down to earth," Julie said. "I think that time in Clarinda became sort of a refuge for him away from the limelight and all the pressure that came with it, a place where he could come, feel comfortable, and just be one of the guys. People in the community have accepted him as one of their own and give him his space. He has become just one more 'Eberly' at the dinner table."

Which would happen frequently. When Hayes needed to get away to do some thinking, sometimes he would get in the car and drive almost all night just to be in Clarinda. "They always had a place for me to stay until I got situated in the area," Hayes said. "They were always accepting."

Even after Hayes built a hunting cabin on his land, Merl and Pat would insist that he stay in town with them. He probably would have had a similar invitation at dozens of houses in town. The people of Clarinda were proud of their association with Hayes and appreciated that he had come back when he was a major league star. Now that he was no longer a celebrity, they embraced him all the same.

The Eberlys' home was the place that brought Hayes peace and renewal, a sense that he could start again. He could relax there and not have to be Von Hayes, professional baseball player. It was that way in town as well. "How he has kept in contact shows what Merl did for him," said John Woolson, whose family owned the *Clarinda Herald-Journal* when Merl worked there. "It was a real influence his whole life. It didn't develop baseball in him. It developed life in him."

13

The Blue Goose

WHEN RYAN EBERLY heard the loud pop from the rear of the bus, he knew there was trouble. His team was riding aboard "Blue Goose IV," the A's bucket of bolts of a bus, in the early morning hours of June 2, 2008, returning from a three-day road trip through Junction City, Kansas, and Topeka, 180 miles from Clarinda. They were ten miles south of St. Joseph, Missouri, on Interstate 29, a little more than an hour from home.

Sometimes Ryan felt like he had spent years of his life on the many versions of the bus, first as a batboy who got handed up and down the rows by the brawny players, then as a player himself who honed his game to the point that he was signed as an infielder by the New York Yankees, and now as the head coach and the person responsible for the twenty-six young men on board. When the sound of the blown tire rang out, at first he thought his biggest challenge would be finding someone to fix a flat after midnight in rural Missouri. He had been through this so many times before.

The various incarnations of the Blue Goose, starting with the original 1946 model donated by a local doctor, Bill Kuehn, in 1974, had broken down so frequently that Ryan and his family had come to accept it as just part of every summer. They joked about being on a first-name basis with the tow truck drivers on the Kansas Turnpike. "There was a feeling about each trip we took that going somewhere in the Blue Goose was no worry, but getting home problem free was something else," Merl wrote in the A's newsletter.

Most of the time the team had a driver, but there were times in the early days when Merl let players drive if they told him they had experience. One of the best player-drivers was Ron Rooker, who had driven trucks and thought buses were easy by comparison. On one trip to South Dakota, the bus broke down just as the team was reaching the motel parking lot. Rooker had forgotten his toolbox, and Merl thought he would have to pay a huge mechanic's bill, but Rooker told him not to worry. Merl went to take a nap in his room, but was woken up by a player telling him that Rooker had all sorts of engine parts on the ground with only a screwdriver and a pair of pliers for tools. "Coach, don't worry about it—I can handle it," Rooker said. And he did, all before pitching the A's to a victory that night.

The A's tried to make the most of the breakdowns, including one time in Emporia, Kansas, where the Blue Goose had stopped running near a restaurant that was offering "one steak supper at regular price, receive the second one free." While they were waiting for the mechanic, Merl asked if the restaurant offer could be applied to his thirty sweaty baseball players, who were more accustomed to roadside fast food after a game. The waitress thought about it for a while, then said yes, the offer stood. The A's filed into the restaurant for one of their better dinners of the summer.

On another trip in the 1970s to Rapid City, South Dakota, a group of young women drove alongside the bus and started flirting with the players, who all rushed to the right side of the bus. One of the women took off her top, prompting a lot more yelling, and Merl covered the eyes of his young son Rodney. Merl thought he had finally persuaded the young women to leave, but when they got to the hotel they found them there already. Merl could tell his players what to do, but these young women did not feel they had to listen to him. "We're just looking for a little fun. No hard feelings, Pop," one of them said to Merl.

"Several of the guys told me not to worry about it and go on to bed and they would handle it for me — I guess they thought this was my first road trip," Merl said. "After turning down the many volunteers who offered to keep an eye on the girls and the rest of the players, I finally made one last effort to break the girls' blockade of the motel by inviting them to come over to the restaurant to eat with us and I would introduce each of the players but they had to introduce themselves too.

"Only two gals showed up, thank goodness. After a small bribe (tip) to the waitress, she agreed to slow our service way down (close to curfew) and the girls decided to leave after they realized I might keep the team there all night if necessary — plus I now had their names and they became uneasy when I asked if their parents knew where they were."

Another time two women who police said had been drinking heavily plowed into the side of the bus with a sickening thud. The crash did more damage to the car, and the Blue Goose was able to make it to the game that night. "That 1946 model was built like a tank," Merl said. The women in the car weren't as fortunate, especially when police saw all the beer cans inside.

Of course there were the stories about how Ozzie Smith and Danny Gans would make the miles go faster by pretending to be the Supremes, with Ozzie doing his best Diana Ross impression. Gans would dazzle his teammates with impressions of the famous and was so adept at it that he would be known in Las Vegas as "the Man of Many Voices." Gans stayed close to the Eberlys and the A's until his death in 2009 and was one of the team's most consistent donors. In fact, it was his contribution that enabled the A's to buy Blue Goose IV, a 1983-model New Jersey Transit bus.

Over the years the various versions of the bus either lacked air conditioning or had it but it often wasn't functioning. All lacked toilets, and none had modern conveniences like a WiFi connection. All of the buses were very old when the A's purchased them and christened them as "new" — that is, new to the A's. As Merl did so often, he made the decidedly downscale transportation a positive part of team lore, starting with the daffy name, the Blue Goose. For the most part, the players put up with the old buses without much complaining, even with all the stiff backs and sore necks that came with riding on them. This "new" version of the Blue Goose had been purchased in 2003, and its amenities included an automatic transmission, power steering, and air conditioning.

In all those years, the problems with the Blue Goose had presented more annoyance than emergency. But in the darkness of the highway that night in rural Missouri, that would change. All that the A's had been would come into sharp focus when it was suddenly at risk.

It was about 12:30 A.M., and most of the players were dozing. Ryan was in his coach's seat near the front of the bus so he could help keep the driver, Charlie Hughes, awake and be a second set of eyes on the road. Michael Ghutzman was among the players sitting near the rear. He was the third in his family to come to Clarinda to play for the A's; his father Butch considered a summer in Clarinda, learning to love the game without amenities, an essential component of a ballplayer's development. After his playing days ended, Michael would become a lawyer in Texas, but meanwhile, he was in Clarinda to pursue his baseball dreams.

For some reason that evening, he stayed awake while all his teammates slept. He heard the rupture of the tire on the rear driver's side — a loud popping sound like the report of a gunshot — and then, to his alarm, he saw sparks flying up from the shredded tire. He called to the front of the bus to alert Charlie and Ryan, who seemed almost indifferent. After all, they had lived through just about every malfunction a bus could have — something wrong with the engine, leaks of all manner of fluids, flat tires, running low on oil and gas. It would take a lot more than a flat tire to get them excited.

They told Ghutzman that it was okay, that the correct thing to do was to keep going to burn the retread off the tire. That didn't seem right to Ghutzman, who feared that the sparks would quickly ignite, possibly even reach the fuel tank. "Ryan and Charlie decided to ignore my plea, and the bus kept on rolling," Ghutzman said.

In the excitement, his teammates had woken up and were now "huddled around the rear windows watching the action," Ghutzman said. Soon they became even more alarmed. "The sparks intensified and flames burst up towards the window.

This development unified my teammates, who now collectively demanded the bus be stopped," Ghutzman said.

As Ryan remembers it, once the players said they saw sparks and small flames, Charlie eased the bus to the side of the road. Ryan said he knew his one responsibility was to get the players off safely. "At the time I was scared to death for the kids," he said. "We got them all off the bus."

Watching his players get safely off the bus, Ryan couldn't help but think about his own days as a player, back when the A's were a constant presence in his life. It started by watching his father play, then his older brother. Players like Ozzie Smith and Von Hayes had become close friends, as well as scores of other former players and coaches. Each summer had brought him twenty new "brothers," most of them as sports-minded as he was. Being around them had made him want to chase the dream of being a major leaguer too.

Ryan had been an outstanding athlete in high school, playing four sports. While he was very good in football, there was little doubt how he would spend each summer—playing baseball, clearly his favorite sport. He had seen his brother Rick get his shot, and he wanted to take his own. Merl never pushed him; Ryan pushed himself hard enough and was never quite satisfied. "You are where you need to be," Merl told his son. "Give it time." Then one summer night in Nevada, Missouri, when he was a high school senior, he proved to be a little ahead of his time. The A's starting shortstop got sick, and Ryan found himself in the starting lineup. From that point on, he knew he had to outwork other players to prove himself. He was from a small town in Iowa with brutal winters, not some year-round baseball climate like so many other heavily recruited players.

Although he played in college and did well, Ryan wasn't drafted, and he thought he would never get the same chance as his father and big brother. He took a coaching job in a town thirty miles west of Clarinda. One night when he came home, Merl handed him a sheet of paper with a phone number on it. His call had come after all, from the New York Yankees. They needed middle infielders, and Ryan had the right pedigree. In two days, he was to report to the Rookie League in Tampa, Florida.

At twenty-three, he was the old man of the group. For some reason, he wasn't getting to play much, and the disappointment hit him hard. "I just didn't understand," Ryan said. "It was very disappointing." Baseball seemed ready to crush the dream of another Eberly. But Ryan was told to stay in good shape and come back for spring training. He got to see players from other major league teams and size himself up against the talent. He thought he was hitting well. Maybe this would happen for him? Then his playing time dropped, and coaches threw him catcher's gear to catch bullpens for pitchers who were rehabilitating from injuries. Ryan now knew his time would be short.

He was called into the manager's office. "You are thinking someone got hurt, and you will get sent somewhere, but then it's like the movie *Bull Durham*, where the coach says, 'This is the toughest part of the job,' and says you are released." The manager told Ryan that he hadn't "graded out" at his position. "My question was, how could you grade me when you weren't playing me? But I got no response. Then in two hours you have to be out of your hotel. You don't really get a definitive answer why."

Ryan knew his father had handled being cut too, and then went on to build the A's program, to not be defined by any perceived failure. He knew Rick had eventually bounced back too.

In fact, having seen Rick go through being released, Ryan said, made it easier for him, even as he noted that baseball is "a dramatic sport" that "really does put a dagger in your heart a lot of times."

The Eberlys had their own way of handling the disappointment of not making it as a pro. "I guess we had something to fall back on and not miss the game," Ryan said. "Some people when they are done playing, they don't want anything to do with it. But it was Dad's influence to want to give back to the game."

After the bus came to a halt, the flames were now more obvious and the heat was intense. On his way off the bus another player, John Fugazi, grabbed the fire extinguisher and did his best to put out the flames. "It looked like I had it, but all of a sudden it reared up," said Fugazi, who had come to the A's from California through a connection to Von Hayes. He told Ryan that the handheld device was no match for a fire that was growing in intensity.

Fugazi had been asleep when the tire blew, but he was fully awake now and watching his baseball gear go up in flames. "It was kind of surreal," he said. "We were sitting there thinking this was just a flat tire . . . The bus driver stayed on the bus until the end. I thought he was going to go down with the ship."

The players stood by helplessly watching as their favorite gloves, bats, iPods, laptops, and phones were lost before their eyes. The ones who had taken their phones off the bus started calling parents to say that they were okay. "As we stood a short distance away down the highway, the fire began to take over the whole of the bus, and the once-proud Blue Goose sat ablaze against the lonely backdrop of the Missouri night's sky," Ghutzman said.

He said it took what seemed like hours before the Faucett Volunteer Fire Department responded to the call, and by that time the bus and its contents were mostly charred rubble. Eventually, police and some local reporters came to the scene as well. When they arrived, the firefighters "began working to put out the fire immediately," Ghutzman said. "When they finally got everything under control, we got the chance to go through some of the stuff in the cargo hold. Generally speaking, the fire destroyed everything. I remember pulling my melted catching gear from my bag. I was only able to salvage one of my mitts, but it was soaked and smelled like smoke. After it dried out a few weeks later, I actually caught a few games with it. It still had the smoky smell, and I referred to it as 'Ole Smoky' for the remainder of the year."

One of the players took a sixteen-second recording with his phone and later posted it on YouTube. A teammate can be heard saying that he can't believe what he is seeing and at the same time plaintively noting that all of the team's equipment is gone, every player's favorite glove and bat, their cleats, the other gear. Gone. Ryan had the painful task of calling Merl and Pat to tell them about the fire. As parents of six children, they knew that no phone call at two in the morning is good news. "Their first response was, 'Is everybody okay?'" Ryan said. "I said, 'Yes, they are not in the greatest mood, but they are okay.'" That had been in no way assured given how fast the fire spread. "Everything happened so fast," Ryan said. "We were on the side of the road for five minutes and in twenty minutes that bus was pretty much gone. That's how fast it happened."

At first, Merl and Pat were in shock. Merl, who had just been diagnosed with cancer a second time, this time in his colon, was scheduled for major surgery in just four days. How could this all be happening at the same time? Then their stoic side prevailed. If everyone was okay, then that was all that was important. Personal effects could be replaced. Pat, as ever, started to think about how to keep the season going, how to organize the schedule, how to talk to the parents who might have concerns, what to tell the players.

The team arranged for a Heartland motor coach to take the players back to Clarinda, where they arrived about 5:00 A.M. "We got back to Clarinda so late, and then said, 'Now what?'" Fugazi said. "What the heck were we going to do?"

Reese McCulley missed the drama. He had arrived in Clarinda to join the team the night of the fire and was long asleep by the time the drama was playing out an hour to the south. McCulley, who was from Oregon, had come to the A's through his coach at Linfield College, Scott Brosius, a former major league star with the Yankees who'd had his own short stint with the A's before he was drafted in 1987. Like so many former players, Brosius had stayed close with the Eberlys and routinely sent them players for summer ball. Brosius wanted McCulley to see how he could do against the higher-level competition that Clarinda offered.

After he woke up, McCulley went to the A's clubhouse at Municipal Stadium to find his teammates and coaches in a state of shock. "There was a lot of burned gear, and guys were airing it out. It smelled bad and people's clothes were stiff and charred." Merl tried to stay positive, telling the players to be patient, that they would work things out.

The players had little idea what Merl was going through. He had surgery on June 6, just five days after the bus fire, and underwent follow-up chemotherapy and radiation that lasted until November. He pretty much shielded the players from his own troubles and focused on them and the field. He counseled Fugazi, who was homesick for his girlfriend, and got him to pay attention to baseball, telling him that the personal relationship, if it was real, would survive a couple months in Iowa. Players saw him as a kindly grandfather who could also have his stern moments if they didn't play the game the right way.

"Between the 1st and the 6th it would have been so easy to just pack it in and cancel the season, but that is where the true essence of the A's program became evident," Pat wrote. "A's board of directors, auxiliary and house parents stepped up, as did the local Chamber of Commerce and our alumni. Before Merl had gone to Omaha for his surgery, we were assured there would be funds to replace the team's shoes, gloves, etc., and that the season would go on as planned."

What happened next was another validation of what Merl and Pat had spent their lives trying to build. Pat said the recovery from the fire underscored for her the "three F's" that were the foundation of the program — faith, family, and friends. The Clarinda Chamber of Commerce called her the next day to offer financial help. Members of the team's board of directors, including Jay Moses, the owner of J's restaurant, stepped up to drive immediately either to Omaha, Des Moines, or Kansas City, to buy replacement equipment. Each player gave the model of his bat and glove that had been lost. The local clothier put in a rush order on new uniform tops; fortunately, the A's had kept some older uniforms back at Municipal Stadium.

Parents of the players sent checks, and insurance money covered some of the loss. Jerry Laverty, an old scout who had worked for several major league teams, contacted his friend Mike Arbuckle, who was then working in the front office for the Philadelphia Phillies. Within days the Phillies sent the Clarinda A's replacement equipment. "Jerry called me and told me what happened and asked us to help take care of as much as we could," Arbuckle said. "It was just the right thing to do. I knew how much Merl and Pat had done to keep things going. This was devastating and out of their control, so we wanted to do what we could to help them."

Donations poured in from former players and their parents. Ozzie Smith and Von Hayes sent contributions. The son of one former player read about the fire and told his dad, who instantly reconnected with the Eberlys and sent a sizable donation. "I knew Clarinda was a very caring and compassionate community," Pat said. "But when you see all of this that came from the outside, you realize that you touched someone. It was verification that you weren't just doing stuff because you were doing it, that it really meant something to other people."

Bill Clark, the old scout who became close friends with the Eberlys, also answered the call, sending catcher's gear and twenty-five dozen baseballs. One former A's player sent a check for $10,000, another sent $5,000. An account was established at the Page County Federal Savings Association to accept donations.

The team laptop computer had been destroyed in the fire, and with it, the statistics up to that point. After the scorebook was eventually found, the stats were brought up to date, using pitcher Steve Szkotak's computer. Donations continued to pour in, even from some of the Japanese tourists who were in Clarinda for the Glenn Miller Festival at the time of the fire. Merl's fear that the team would have to borrow money to keep operations going proved unfounded.

For the team, the fire ended up helping to unify them. "It loosens you up," McCulley said. "After it happens, you laugh about it. There's nothing you can do about it. And when you start laughing with your teammates and interacting, you get more comfortable and it just makes for a more enjoyable summer. Baseball becomes a different game, and everything started jelling and happening easier on the field."

Merl, even distracted by illness, inspired the players with stories about Ozzie Smith. "Just having Merl talk about that gave all of us hoping to have that professional career a glimmer of hope." McCulley returned to Oregon a better pitcher, having played against the better players in Clarinda. "It was big because it gave me that opportunity. You faced that kind of competition, so it gives you confidence that going forward, this is possible. I can get these guys out. I think it played a huge role in my development. If I hadn't gone to Clarinda and played baseball that summer, maybe there would be some doubt in my mind. I think all of us appreciate what the Eberlys did. It was not like they were making hundreds of thousands of dollars off the team. They were instilling values through the game of baseball."

But as his college career came to a close, McCulley wasn't drafted by a major league team. He took a job as an intern for the Salem Volcanoes, the minor league team in Salem, Oregon, near his hometown of Keizer, Oregon, which at the time was managed by Tom Trebelhorn, who also had managed in the majors for the Cubs and Brewers. McCulley, whose job was to help with the operational side of things, had his eye on finding some kind of job in baseball.

The Volcanoes were scheduled to play a preseason game just before the start of official league play. Trebelhorn didn't want to burn one of his regular pitchers, and he knew that McCulley had pitched in college. So he did the unthinkable: he asked the intern to suit up. McCulley threw "very well," and so Trebelhorn continued to have him work out with the team, throwing bull-pen sessions on the side during the day while working games at night. The Giants then offered McCulley a contract, and he was sent to the Rookie League in Arizona. There he pitched only three and a third innings, giving up three earned runs while striking out eight. But he forever after had the credential of being a professional baseball player.

In that summer of 2008, McCulley and his teammates had a winning season and made it to the NBC tournament in Wichita. Despite the fire, the team had missed only one game. The Clarinda A's, which had given so many players their shot, was now getting a second chance in return. On June 23, the A's hit the road again in a "new" bus, "Blue Goose V" — a 1994 Greyhound.

14

Heading Home

M ERL HAD SPENT his time as a baseball player practic-
ing indifference to pain. He had seen plenty of blood in
his life, from his fights in his youth, on his hunting trips, and
throughout his years on the baseball diamond. He had endured
nagging injuries and the aches that came more frequently as he
hit his seventies. He just wasn't one to complain.

He also wasn't one who liked to make visiting his doctor a
habit. But in April 2007, he went in for a routine physical and
came away with a diagnosis of prostate cancer. A man whose life
in many ways had been defined by his physicality was now vul-
nerable. For treatment, he chose a hormone therapy over surgery for a simple reason: he didn't want his condition to affect
the A's that summer. When the season ended, he had surgery,
and his doctors pronounced him cured — another win for the
man who lived for competition.

Just a year later, though, in the spring of 2008, he began to
have some troubling symptoms, and doctors discovered a large
mass in his lower colon. He couldn't postpone surgery this time.

On June 1, just days before his operation, he had taken his son Ryan's predawn phone call about the fire on the Blue Goose. There were so many things to think about as Merl tried to ready himself for major surgery at Clarkson Hospital in Omaha. He and Pat made the drive, anxious but resolved. Afterward, the doctors pronounced the operation a success, but told Merl he would need chemotherapy and radiation. Three weeks into the treatment, Merl told his oncologist that something "didn't feel right," but he was encouraged to continue to get the full twenty-eight days, and the doctors said he was doing well. So well, in fact, that they gave Merl approval to go on a pheasant-hunting trip in South Dakota with his sons and grandsons in October. Von Hayes joined them, along with a couple of other former players. Merl was able to walk with them in the morning, but rode with the guide in the afternoon.

The treatments had been debilitating, causing far more pain that he had ever experienced. It got so bad that Pat felt the need to schedule an appointment with the family doctor, Bill Richardson. The day of the appointment she heard Merl moving about upstairs and told him to "hurry up" because it was almost time to leave. Merl said he didn't feel like going. Pat said, "Merl James Eberly, either you are going with me or I am calling the ambulance." Merl relented.

Bill Richardson, whose efforts at a high school track meet Merl had mercilessly criticized decades before, was now helping to keep Merl, who had become a valued friend, alive. After examining him, he admitted Merl to the hospital and ordered intravenous fluids to reverse severe dehydration. The next day, November 11, 2008, Merl was taken by ambulance to Bergan Mercy Hospital in Omaha.

He was getting worse and felt like his doctors weren't listening to him. When Merl's oncologist came to see him, Merl looked up, grabbed his jacket, pulled him down to the bed, and said, "From now on, please listen to older patients. They know what their bodies are telling them." The doctor said he had no idea there was so much damage because Merl had appeared to be such a big, strong man.

Pat could tell that Merl was also getting depressed, so she spoke to him as only she could. "I gave him a hug and told him, 'I know you're not feeling good, but you just have to suck it up and deal with it.'" Merl would later recount the story to friends and joke about what a "compassionate" wife he had.

Early on the morning of November 19, Merl said he saw an angel at the foot of his bed and told Pat later that his first thought was, *I've got to quit using this morphine pump so much.* Still, he said, a feeling of calm had washed over him at that moment. Merl was raised to study the Bible and usually read it every day, though he was not a regular churchgoer.

The next day was a flurry of medical procedures, and Merl was failing quickly. His surgeon came in at 9:00 A.M. and told Merl he would be operating on him that afternoon at 2:30. "If you could bring me back to this room, I would be eternally grateful," Merl said. "If not, that's all right too."

Merl made it through surgery, and he was able to go back to his home on Lincoln Street on December 5. "We really didn't think he would make it, and I knew he felt the same way," Pat said. "When we got home and he got upstairs to his own bed, he cried and cried, saying he never thought he would come back home."

By Christmas, Merl, though still weak, had recovered to the point that he could once again play Santa for his younger grand-children and great-grandchildren. More chemotherapy seemed to keep the cancer in check, and he was able to enjoy another A's season in 2009. Each summer brought its own special joy, with the sounds and rhythms of the game and the chance to see old friends at the ballpark. For the first six months of 2010, Merl and Pat had reason to hope, and he was seen around town as the two of them busily prepared for another season. Then, in the middle of 2010, a second oncologist told Merl that his cancer had spread to his liver, on multiple spots — a most troubling sign.

He had beaten back disease now for the better part of three years, but this was different. He was just so tired, though it raised his spirits when he heard from his former players or old friends. As word of his worsening condition spread, the calls to the old coach were increasing.

Andrew Cashner, the pitcher from Texas sent to him by his college coach and former A's player Jeff Livin, had become the polished pitcher Merl thought he could be. He had been signed by Merl's beloved Chicago Cubs and was pitching at the time for the team's Triple A affiliate in Des Moines. With Merl in decline, Ryan called Cashner to tell him of his condition. Cashner was soon in his car to drive the two hours to Clarinda. There he met up with Merl in the dugout at Municipal Stadium.

When Cashner arrived in Clarinda in the summer of 2006, he had been more potential than real prospect. Tall and lean but obviously strong, he had a live arm and a confident manner on the mound. He had only started pitching in his senior year of high school and had thrown just twenty innings during his freshman season in college. He could throw ninety-five miles an hour, but didn't always know where the ball was going. Livin thought a summer in Clarinda might be just the thing to refine Cashner's obvious athletic gifts.

He drove up from Texas with a teammate, and like a lot of players who came to Clarinda, he kept asking, "Are we ever going to get there?" Finally, they arrived, and it was time for Cashner to find out where he stood.

But he almost never got to find out. Only two weeks after he arrived in Clarinda, Cashner was driving his red truck back to the home of Brian and Laurie Brockman, his host family, on a dark, rain-slicked road on the edge of town. As he approached a bridge, Cashner lost control of the truck and it plummeted off the bridge and into a creek. When police arrived, they expected the worst. But Cashner had survived. He was somehow able to extract himself from his pickup, walk to a house nearby, and call the Brockmans. He told police that he had fallen asleep. Later he conceded that he might have "had a little help" falling asleep.

For Merl and Pat, the well-being of the players was always the first concern. In all their years with the A's, there had been injuries and trips to the emergency room, but nothing even close to this. "I was very lucky to be alive," Cashner said. "I remember Merl, after that happened, was teary-eyed and gave me a big hug. He didn't say much. He was just happy to know I was alive."

Cashner had his second chance. Though some in town were dubious of the notion that he had fallen asleep, he was allowed to stay on the team. "I think after that, it kind of changed, the whole summer changed baseball for me. It opened up my eyes on life, to kind of slow down a little. It was a wake-up period, to not take life for granted, to not take baseball for granted. That summer taught me about life. Everybody who saw my truck couldn't believe I had lived."

His host family helped him get through the gossip in town

about the nature of the accident. "The Brockmans just treated me like one of their own kids ... You make mistakes and you move forward and try not to make the same mistake twice."

When Cashner was pitching and would come off the field, Merl would often stop him, from his perch near the clubhouse door, to review the game. "If we stunk it up, he let you know," Cashner said. "He never held his opinion. He gave his opinion. There was no sugarcoating. It was the truth. But he was very quiet. His answers were always very well thought out. He might be mad, but he was never yelling mad." Ryan Eberly, Cashner's coach, had learned to pass on some baseball wisdom just like Merl. "Ryan always said, 'Catch the ball with two hands until you make the first million,'" Cashner said. "That always stuck in my head."

In the dugout in the summer of 2010, Merl and Cashner reflected on the accident and how it had affected both of their lives. They talked about Cashner turning into a truly complete pitcher that summer, learning from the other pitchers and becoming more dedicated and serious about what he was doing, more able to focus and think, not just throw. Merl also drew Cashner out about other aspects of his life. Merl was different that way from a lot of coaches who only cared about performance on the field. Merl asked about a player's background and how he got into baseball; he wanted to know about a player's family and about his dreams.

They talked about hand-fishing and pheasant hunting, and of course they also talked about baseball. "He was asking questions about where I was, what I was going through, the ride, did I ever think I would be where I was? He told me how proud he was. He wasn't in the best shape when I saw him, but he was still getting around. He was never going to show what he was going through. I just remember he had a hard time walking out of the dugout."

While Merl was a man of strong opinions, he was rarely given to self-analysis, or at least not in ways that he often shared. But this was a time of rare introspection for Merl. As his illness took a stronger grip on him, he started sharing thoughts with his oldest daughter, Julie, in a journal. He wanted to make sure that he left some things said, not unsaid.

"I try to lead a clean life and do what I say I will do," Merl said. "I don't always get it done, but that's what I strive to do. I think I am pretty reliable, at least most of the time, and most of all I hope that I have been a good provider for my family as well as a good husband and father to my children. A good family man. If I have done that, then what else could I hope for?

"Caring about other people, regardless of class status — in this world today everyone seems to be trying to outdo their neighbors. Being a good American has always been something I feel strongly about and honoring those who kept us free — some gave their all at a very young age. I thank God each and every day I am alive and hopefully beyond. I have a lot of respect for the senior citizens of our country, and hopefully I have given back for the help I received growing up. Trying to be a good person is what I am saying and having others respect that."

He told his daughter that he had few regrets in life, though he would have liked to take a trip to Normandy to see what the brave soldiers faced on D-Day during World War II. "I will always have that feeling, even today, that those who served their country allowed me to live a free and full life. I have been blessed with family . . . [with] the things freedom allows because of their sacrifice. I just thought that would have been something that I had a great desire to do. God bless them all!"

He also talked about the people he looked up to, including his old coaches John Tedore and Al Gray, men who had seen potential in him and given him a second chance. He admired Delmar Haley, the country hardball player who later worked as an umpire at A's games. He appreciated his uncles, Ben Eberly and Lawrence Barchus, who had taught him to hunt and respect nature, as well as his stepfather, Stanley Zdan, and Vernon Hamilton, a man who had built his own business in Clarinda from scratch.

When he was a young man, very little had been expected of Merl. But he had proved his doubters wrong, and in ways not even he could fully realize. Why did Merl do it? Why did he spend all those hours on baseball? On organizing the team and raising money, for other people's children, with no compensation? "It was just part of who he was," Julie said. "And he didn't think of it as toil. There were never too many miles to drive to play a game or too many doors to open to put a team on the field. He loved the game . . . the competition. He had a strong sense of community, and sports were what he knew, and a way through which he could contribute. It just kind of seems like it was a progression from him playing to people hearing about the program — to him coaching and becoming a mentor. I'm sure at some level he saw it as an opportunity to give back by providing the same opportunity to others.

"If he was overcompensating, then he did it effortlessly — at least in my eyes — to be able to keep up a full-time job, raise a family, be involved in community activities, and still do all it took to put the A's on the field year after year," Julie said. "On some levels, I'm not sure he saw the missteps of his youth as anything more than a stepping-stone and learning experience which led him to where he was supposed to be."

Though his regrets were few, he did lament not trying to do more to stop the sale of the newspaper — not to save his own job so much as to save the jobs of others and preserve the role the paper played in the community.

Merl had more good days than bad, at least to those around him. He stayed mostly in his home, in the bedroom upstairs on Lincoln Street, visiting with a parade of people whose lives he had impacted in such a profound and positive way. One of them was his old teammate and coaching buddy Milan Shaw. The two of them had been through so much together, and these visits were difficult for them both. "Merl was one of those people — baseball was his whole identity," Shaw said.

But Merl also went on to build something much larger for his town and his team, repaying Clarinda for helping to redeem him. "Some people can take this road or that road," Shaw said. "He could have said, 'I had a terrible life, so I am not worried about anyone else.' He went the other route. He was going to rectify all of the mistakes and things he had missed out on in his life."

Merl was fixated on one last project for the A's — raising money for a new scoreboard. Along with a form letter sent to A's alumni seeking donations, he insisted on writing personal notes. He would write ten to fifteen a day before tiring. He had things he wanted to finish. But as he was nearing the end, he was sleeping much of the time, his body racked with pain.

"Life is a great go-around, and as I have gotten older I have begun to understand even more how it works," Merl said. "Sure, as you know, there are ups and downs, but thank the good Lord we all seem to have more of the ups. I think you should also know, if you don't already, that the best things in life are free but do require some work to achieve, and last, if you don't know, your dad was very competitive in just about everything he tried to do — second was just not good enough."

As competitive as Merl was, he was also a realist. Not long after the New Year in 2011, he decided to stop his treatments. They were too debilitating. "He knew the time he had left was limited, and he wanted to feel as good as he could for as long as he could," Pat said. She continued to get things organized for the season, making sure players had been contacted, scheduling games and umpires, ordering supplies for the concession stand, all the while caring for her husband.

They were able to work in a trip to Texas, where the team Rick coached, Highland Community College in Kansas, had traveled for games. Merl had another motivation: to make amends with a half-brother from whom he had been estranged. The day before they were to leave for Texas, Merl blacked out, but he insisted that Pat not tell their children. He needed the closure with John Mark Eberly, and nothing was going to stop him from making the drive.

In Texas the two brothers talked to each other and repaired their breach. Merl and Pat also were able to see some former players and their parents, and Merl's spirits were up as they made their way back to Clarinda, just before the start of another season.

Merl and Pat tried to maintain their normal routines, but that was becoming increasingly difficult. Merl told Pat he wanted to make it at least until July 4, the annual parents' weekend for A's players. Merl always enjoyed meeting the parents, and he often gave a short talk at a luncheon put on by the women's auxiliary. The previous year the luncheon was held in a large room at Clarinda Lutheran School, near the edge of town. At rows of tables, hungry players sat side by side with their host parents and their real ones. Each player introduced himself, along with his hosts and his family. Players then went into the gymnasium for a team photo of the entire A's family.

Merl had one more speech to the faithful in him, and even with a somewhat weakened voice, he could still command the room. He held a microphone and talked in his soothing lilt about the history of the program and what it meant to players and the town. He joked that while he was quite capable of giving players instruction, he most often chose not to, so as not to incur the wrath of their college coaches.

The next year Merl and Pat were able to celebrate their birthdays on May 12 and 13 and also have a Mother's Day weekend with family at Julie's lake house about an hour away. The family time was restorative, if only temporarily so. Merl was able to speak at length with all of his children and grandchildren.

It seemed like every day now Merl would receive another letter or phone call from a former player or coach. The 2011 A's players started arriving on May 22, and Merl was able to greet several of them along with their parents. He was also able to spend time with some of the people whose lives he had shaped just by their association with the A's. He talked to Jeff Clark during one of his last trips to the field, going over what in effect was his to-do list for improvements to the field. He knew Clark would do his best to see that they were done. "He told me he was proud of me, and I about started crying," Clark said. "It meant a lot to me because of all he had done in his life. It meant a whole lot."

On May 26, the A's held their annual youth clinic, where that summer's team gave lessons to kids in town. Pat and Jill had gone down to the field to get the concession stand ready for the A's opener in three days. Julie and Rick's wife, Angie, stayed with Merl at the house on Lincoln Street. He had spent days in his bedroom, greeting a stream of visitors. His family rarely left him alone.

Angie decided to join the others at Municipal Stadium and take photos of her five-year-old, Cooper, at his first A's clinic. Cooper was considered a bit of a miracle, as Rick and Angie had difficulty conceiving and had almost given up. Cooper was a constant source of joy for Merl, particularly during this period of grave illness. Merl seemed to be sleeping comfortably, so Julie left to return to her home near Des Moines. Pat and Jill told each other they would go get Merl "in a few minutes."

Merl awoke and had enough strength to be angry. Where was everyone? Adrenaline propelled him to sit up and eventually to walk down the creaky oak stairs. He knew he wanted to see his grandson at the clinic, another generation of the Eberlys taking up the game. He gathered himself further, grabbed his car keys, and headed into the garage. He started the car and drove to the field, a trip he had made several thousand times in his life.

When he walked in front of the concession stand, Pat shouted, "Merl James Eberly, did you drive down here by yourself?" He glowered back and said, "What was I supposed to do when everyone had abandoned me?" Then, as he looked toward the field, he saw his five-year-old grandson beginning his own journey with the game Merl so loved. The man who rarely cried had tears in his eyes.

Unbeknownst to the rest of the family, Merl had already discussed his condition with Cooper. Angie had told the boy they were going to Iowa from their home in Kansas because his grandpa wasn't feeling well. Cooper said he understood. Every morning Cooper would go to Merl's room, look out the west window, and tell him what was going on, silly stories like, "That black squirrel of yours is chasing the red one," and important stories like the one about hooking his first catfish and his accounts of the previous night's A's game.

Cooper's sweet perspective on such a grim situation helped the whole family as they began a final vigil. The house on Lincoln Street had been home since August 1960, and their large family was intact, even growing closer at this time.

A few days later, Merl wanted to go to the A's home opener but couldn't make it down the stairs, not even with the help of one of his sons. It was the first time either he or Pat had missed an opening game in more than three decades.

By June 1, his family had gathered again in Clarinda to be with him, to help Pat, and to try to come to a place of closure. Their presence ensured that Merl could stay at home. Dr. Richardson came by to check on him, not for treatment, but just to talk. His oncologist stopped by as well. Even to his doctors, Merl was special.

It was clear that his remaining time was short. Pat decided to call people who might want to see Merl a final time, and one of the first on her list was Ozzie Smith. When she contacted him, Smith dropped everything and headed to the airport to catch a flight to Kansas City, about a two-hour drive from Clarinda. Merl had meant so much to him, and the arc of their lives had been so interwoven, the young black man from Los Angeles coming to find himself as a baseball player with the old-school white coach in the cornfields. He would do whatever it took to see Merl one last time.

Baseball was the lens through which Ozzie and Merl saw each other, not race. It was in Clarinda that Smith realized that if he worked hard enough — which meant outworking everyone else — he would have a shot, and he never forgot who helped to get him there. His eyes were also opened during his time in Clarinda to what he called "people who were of the land," people who in his mind had a special set of values.

One of the greatest validations Merl could draw from those decades with the A's was the enduring nature of his relationship with Smith. They celebrated Smith's triumphs in baseball, from his first contract in San Diego to his Hall of Fame speech in Cooperstown, New York, on July 28, 2002, with Merl and Pat in the front row. Their conversations were free and easy, no matter how much time had passed between them. While their backgrounds could hardly have been more different, their bond was unshakable. In the thirty-six years of their relationship, so many things in the world had changed, and so many of them for the better. The Soviet Union had crumbled. America had elected a black president, and it was winning the Iowa caucuses that had sent Barack Obama on his way. Ozzie Smith, a kid from Watts, was a Hall of Famer and still a national celebrity.

For Merl and Ozzie, fame was the least of it. Their friendship was forged in baseball, but it went well beyond the field. As Smith was racing to make it to Clarinda, he was replaying his time with Merl — that first day when Merl thought he might break him only to see the kind of steel that his skinny shortstop was made of; the games in Alaska and at the NBC tournament; then the games with the Cardinals, including playoffs and World Series. He thought about his talks with Merl on the phone, too many to count, and all those conversations that were about everything but baseball. He also recalled all the trips he had made back to Clarinda to sign autographs and raise money for the team at its annual Hall of Fame Banquet — journeys he had made, often on twisting two-lane highways, because of his fealty to the Eberlys. The baseball superstar felt as at home on Lincoln Street as he did anywhere on earth.

He pulled into town on Glenn Miller Avenue, drove past the courthouse with the monument to Vernon Baker, past Weil's clothing store, Taylor Pharmacy, and J's restaurant, all so very much as it was in the summer of 1975. Ozzie Smith was not of these people, but these were his people.

When Smith was inducted into the Baseball Hall of Fame, he made sure the baseball world knew of his path through Clarinda and its lasting importance in his life. "I will forever cherish the life-changing experience and strands of love that I was blessed with through my relationship with Merl and Pat Eberly while playing semipro baseball in Clarinda, Iowa," Smith said in his speech that day. "Merl and Pat are also here today. Thank you. You know, most people would have no idea of how intimidating and stressful it could be for a young black player to move into an all-white, rural community in the Midwest. However, Merl and Pat took me in and taught me how to live with that challenge. As my coach, Merl taught me the value of strict discipline and the importance of constantly improving my game. And I would be remiss if I didn't take the time to thank that entire community of Clarinda, Iowa, for the strands of love and friendship they showed me then and still do today."

Memories of those summers and of the dozens of visits that followed came back to him as he turned right onto Lincoln and pulled up to the white frame house on the corner, the one with a home plate for a doormat. He had walked through that front door so many times that he was as familiar with it as he was with his own home. He greeted Pat, the woman whose irrepressible spirit had nurtured him as well, and then he headed up the oak stairs.

He made it just in time to see Merl, who always ended his phone calls to Smith with, "I love you, man." Merl had been in and out of consciousness and not really able to hold a conversation for days. "You don't know what to say and sometimes it's not about saying anything as much as it is just being there," Smith said. The old coach looked up at his most famous player and managed a broad smile. "Hey, Oz, good to see you," Merl said.

It was one of the last conscious moments of Merl's life. He died five days later, at 4:30 in the morning. Pat contacted family members who weren't there, and they gathered for an embrace. Later they sat around the kitchen table to discuss what to do about the A's doubleheader that night. There was really no doubt. The games went on.

Afterword

You still feel Merl Eberly at Municipal Stadium. You still see what he built. There is the press stand that always needs another coat of paint after a harsh Iowa winter. There are the advertisements, lining the outfield fence, for Hy-Vee, the grocery store, and Ding's Honk 'n' Holler, a drive-up beverage store. There is the scoreboard, finally, a newer electronic version that Merl had made a minor obsession. There is the sign that now proclaims MUNICIPAL STADIUM, HOME OF EBERLY FIELD, so that Merl's name will always be associated with the place. Beyond the right-field fence, there is corn in the even-numbered years, soybeans in the odd ones. There are rectangular plaques on the side of the concession stand to honor the A's who made it to the major leagues — three dozen and counting. Another sign honors the 1981 champions, listing each player and his college. And now there is the bronze bust of Merl that Ozzie Smith commissioned and presented to the Eberly family, a work of art at Merl's field.

Smith surprised Pat and her family with the bust at the A's

annual Hall of Fame Banquet in 2012. A family not readily given to tears let them pour forth. The bust is an extraordinary likeness of Merl, smiling, wearing a Clarinda A's baseball hat. "I knew it would be something that would live on forever," Smith told the *Herald-Journal*. "I knew it was something that Mrs. E and Ryan and the whole family would love. I wanted them to have a place to go where they could touch and feel it, and hopefully preserve some history."

For Smith, the Eberlys remain a pleasant bridge to his past and an important part of his present. Sitting in the Eberlys' family room in a recliner, he said, "All you have to do is come here. It's home. They made us all feel like part of the family. It was always open. There was love among their family that all of us wish and hope for in our own lives."

On January 5, 2013, at the American Baseball Coaches Association convention, Pat walked as the lone woman in a long line of men whose work in the game was to be honored. All of her children were there, her three sons (looking somewhat uncomfortable wearing suits), her three daughters, her oldest grandson, B.J., his brother Johnny, and her youngest, Cooper.

Tim Corbin, the head coach at Vanderbilt, introduced Pat to receive the association's Meritorious Service Award on behalf of her late husband. It was an honor that had gone to Mike Scioscia and Dave Winfield the year before, and to Nolan Ryan and Cal Ripken Jr. in prior years. Merl Eberly, a man little known outside his hometown save in the larger fraternity of baseball, was in rarefied company. Now his name was listed among legends of the game. He hadn't been much for ceremony, but he certainly would have enjoyed this.

One of his former players, Stacey Burkey, was in the audience as a coach in his twenty-fifth year at Three Rivers College.

When he was playing in Clarinda, Burkey said he was always trying to make an impression so Merl "would say something to me." Merl was never too high or too low on the field, and Burkey had tried to adopt that approach. Merl advised him to always show his players that he cared about them. "They will put out a full effort if they know you care," Merl told him. He finds himself exhorting his players just as Merl did. "Hobby Dobby!"

Pat rose to speak, uncomfortable at first, uncharacteristically emotional in front of several thousand coaches, but she soon righted herself. "Coaches played a very big part in his becoming the man that he did," Pat said. The message Merl took from sports, she said, was to "try to be a little better person tomorrow than you are today. Care for and respect others, and whatever you do, do it with passion and for the right reasons.

"This is the first time I have been able to publicly thank you, the coaches who sent us the boys of summer . . . you are not just teaching athletic skills. You are touching the lives of young men in so many other ways, and as he did, please continue to pay it forward."

A number of people in Clarinda doubted that the A's could survive Merl's death, and more than a few questioned whether Ryan could handle the manager duties. But there Ryan is, night after night, hitting ground balls, throwing batting practice, coaching third base. In 2013 the Clarinda A's won the MINK League title, and Ryan Eberly was named Manager of the Year.

Pat and her family will try to keep the A's going for as long as there are players eager to play summer ball and fans eager to watch them.

Acknowledgments

This book could not have happened without Pat Eberly, one of the most relentlessly optimistic people I have ever met. Her help on the book, as researcher, broker of contacts, fact-checker, and provider of invaluable photos and archives, enlivens almost every page. She has been even more vital to the success of the Clarinda A's.

The other person essential to this book is my son Lee, whose own journey through Clarinda showed me up close what a special place it is. My wife Julie remains my most critical and helpful editor, a life partner in every sense whose Iowa roots gave me a special connection. My daughter Kate provided constant encouragement and never stopped believing in the story's potential.

My sisters, Mary Ann Wildman and Barbara Vetor, both teachers, were helpful readers, and my eagle-eyed mother-in-law, Jean Carey, was invaluable as well.

So many former A's players were generous with their time and provided such rich detail that made this baseball era vivid.

I am particularly indebted to Ozzie Smith, Von Hayes, Buddy Black, Darrell Miller, Andy Benes, Jamey Carroll, Cal Eldred and Andrew Cashner. The A's proved that baseball also is a family, and the many members of the A's family — both in Clarinda and around the country — helped me complete the story. The people of Clarinda also helped me understand their town and why the A's were such an integral part of it. The Devoe family will always hold a place in our hearts.

I must also single out my great friend James Warren, who knows this manuscript at least as well as I do and whose care, time, and editing talent took the story to another level. Others who helped me shape the book include Wes Kosova, who was the inspiration for the title, David Maraniss, whose insight shaped the narrative arc, and Amanda Bennett, who pushed me to take on this project. Many others provided wonderful feedback, including Phil Mattingly, Luke Albee, Jeff Zeleny, Jim Clark, Kerry Luft, Mark Rohner, and Evan Osnos. Thank you also to Nell Minow, who offered encouragement when it was needed most.

This book would not have been launched without the peerless professionalism of David Black and his colleague David Larabell, who took a chance on a first-time author and found this book a great home at Houghton Mifflin Harcourt, where I owe a great debt to a sparkling editor, Susan Canavan. Her careful eye and wise counsel elevated the story at almost every turn.

I only met Merl Eberly once, long enough to shake his hand and say thank you. I hope this book honors the man, the town, and the team.

Index

254 · *Index*